DESIGN
For Your Mind

HOW A FAMILY CAREGIVER AND MENTAL HEALTH
THERAPIST RENOVATED HER HOME TO RECHARGE HER LIFE—
AND DIDN'T BREAK THE BANK.

ANNIE GUEST

B.D. WALSH
PUBLISHING LLC

Text and photo copyright © 2025 by B. D. Walsh Publishing LLC

All rights reserved. No part of this book may be reproduced in any form without written permission from the publisher.

Printed by B. D. Walsh Publishing LLC, in Pittsburgh, PA

First printing, 2025

Library of Congress Control Number: 2024926489
Published in Pittsburgh, PA

979-89922033-2-5 (paperback)
979-89922033-3-2 (hardcover)
979-89922033-4-9 (IngramSpark hardcover)
979-8-9922033-5-6 (limited edition hardcover)
979-8-9922033-1-8 (ebook)

B. D. Walsh Publishing LLC
429 Fourth Avenue
Pittsburgh, PA 15219
info@bdwalshpublishing.com

All photographs by Annie Guest, unless otherwise credited
Cover and book design by Renata Strauss of madegraphicdesign.com
Editing by Clare Wood and Beth Butler of selfpublishingservices.com
Front cover image by Taylor B. Cartwright
Marketing and asset wrangling by Melanie Calahan of selfpublishingservices.com
Project management and publicity by Margaret Genevich of selfpublishingservices.com
Proofreading and indexing by Anna Krusinski http://editsbyanna.wordpress.com

To learn more about design to support mental health,
visit www.annieguestdesignforyourmind.com.

Front cover: Mark Rothko Reproduction, Blue, Orange, Red Canvas by StoneofArts (etsy.com). Throw pillows: Delancey embroidered throw pillow (Pottery Barn); Thibaut Austin striped pillow in blue by PillowFever (etsy.com); and indigo blue velvet pillow by LovePillowArt (etsy.com). Sofa: Rencher sofa and chaise by Mercury Row.

DISCLAIMER

The information presented in this book is offered for educational purposes only and is not intended as a substitute for professional counseling or therapy. Readers are advised not to use this book to diagnose or treat any psychological or medical condition. If you are struggling with your mental health, please seek guidance from qualified professionals whose responsibility it is to determine your condition and provide you with appropriate treatment and personalized support.

You may find resources available at
https://www.nimh.nih.gov/health/find-help

Or you may find the right therapist for you at:
psychologytoday.com
goodtherapy.org
or openpathcollective.org

DEDICATION

To my brother David.

In the midst of hate, I found there was,
within me, an invincible love.

In the midst of tears, I found there was,
within me, an invincible smile.

In the midst of chaos, I found there was,
within me, an invincible calm…

In the midst of winter, I found there was,
within me, an invincible summer.

—Albert Camus

And to Kathy Mosgovoy O'Dell.

To be what we are,
and to become what we are capable of becoming,
is the only end of life.

—Robert Louis Stevenson

ACKNOWLEDGMENTS

Everywhere I look in this house, I see the dedication and ingenuity that Kurt T. brought to its renovation. We faced some novel challenges, and Kurt tackled each one with his characteristic enthusiasm and resourcefulness. Whether he was tapping into his own broad experience, doing research online, or holding after-hours consultations with similarly talented friends, Kurt figured out how to get the job done. Kurt is a big reason this vision came to life.

Friends and family influenced this book in myriad ways—always, I assert, for the better. They read drafts, advised on subtitles, and opined on design ideas. Every one of their insights found its way into the book. But the prize nugget in all of this input, the *sine qua non* of support, has been their enthusiasm for the book and their words of encouragement.

Stepping into the unknown is not for sissies (I like to think), and to be rooted for as one does it is a precious thing. My friend Bethany Cartwright has supported this book and cheered me on since I scribbled the first words on loose-leaf paper in a three-ring binder. It has been a thrill to brainstorm with my fellow author L. M. Snowe and to navigate the writing and publishing world together as we both worked on our first books.

I owe a deep debt to Laura Green King, Lisa Jones, Alicia Schmitt, Jackie Gabrielson Fein, Rick Otte, Heather Semple, Cecily Marble, Cindy Scheel Rus, Stephanie Sajjadieh, Maia Clavin, my sister-in-law Kate, and the late Kathy Mosgovoy O'Dell, for reading and commenting, but mostly, for being excited about the book. I thank my sister Manny for being proud of me and for saying so.

Finally, I could not have taken this book to a better editor than Clare Wood. She guided its progress without stepping on my prose or meddling in anything I was trying to say. Renata Strauss's work on the design and layout dazzled me. This was *not* an easy book to put together. Melanie Calahan is a sure-footed, confident, marketing whiz. I have loved learning from her.

In the end, this book has taught me that support matters. It sustains, it guides, it inspires, it heals. I don't plan to take it for granted, whether I'm on the receiving end again next time or I have the opportunity to offer it.

What Reviewers are Saying...

"As an integrative neurologist specializing in chronic conditions, I witness the profound physical and emotional toll caregiving imposes on my patients and their families. This book...not only acknowledges the unique challenges caregivers face, but also provides practical strategies for creating environments that foster healing, balance, and mental clarity."

Sushma Kola, MD, Director of Integrative Neurosciences, Movement Disorders Specialist, Allegheny Health Network, Pittsburgh, PA

"...[A]ccessible suggestions that combine beauty and functionality, making them achievable even for those with limited time or resources... [A] powerful reminder that small, thoughtful changes in our surroundings can significantly enhance our ability to care for others—and ourselves."

Sushma Kola, MD, Director of Integrative Neurosciences, Movement Disorders Specialist, Allegheny Health Network, Pittsburgh, PA

"With personal anecdotes, practical guides, evidence-based insights, and a touch of humor, it delivers an effortless and enjoyable read. Annie Guest makes a significant contribution to the fields of both caregiving and design, offering a fresh perspective on how our environments can foster resilience and well-being."

Sushma Kola, MD, Director of Integrative Neurosciences, Movement Disorders Specialist, Allegheny Health Network, Pittsburgh, PA

"[The] 'before and after' photos... vividly showcase how changes in furniture arrangement, color psychology, texture, lighting, and nature integration can convert a dull room into one of purpose and sanctuary."

Sushma Kola, MD, Director of Integrative Neurosciences, Movement Disorders Specialist, Allegheny Health Network, Pittsburgh, PA

"We follow Guest's journey as she declutters, repurposes, and redecorates, incorporating mid-century, global, and contemporary elements—including playful blues, greens and pinks, ikat patterns, contemporary reproductions and boucle and jute textures—to complement the existing traditional pieces. Her process demonstrates how to honor existing elements while creating a space that reflects individual needs and preferences. This is a valuable lesson for homeowners seeking to personalize their spaces without resorting to wholesale renovations."

Anne Willoughby, Designer
PorchLight Home Interior Designs

"Annie Guest's book, *Design for Your Mind,* is a treasure to keep and to share."

Lisa C. Krueger, Ph.D., Clinical Psychologist and Poet
Floriography Child

"As an experienced caregiver and mental health therapist, Guest offers creative yet practical approaches to envisioning new ways of living and being."

Lisa C. Krueger, Ph.D., Clinical Psychologist and Poet
Floriography Child

"…[O]ffers a unique awareness of research on both psychological challenges and resources."

Lisa C. Krueger, Ph.D., Clinical Psychologist and Poet
Floriography Child

"Rather than gut original design elements, Guest figures out how to embrace them and blend them with new elements that reflect her own personal style. The reader can literally feel the grand old house shake off its lingering sadness and become a sanctuary of hope, renewal and positive energies."

Gina Leatherman, Author
What Does a Friend Look Like?

CONTENTS

DISCLAIMER

DEDICATION

ACKNOWLEDGMENTS

WHAT REVIEWERS ARE SAYING...

PREFACE

INTRODUCTION

WHY DESIGN? 2
A Room of One's Own 4
Why We Need Personal Space 4
We Also Need One Another 6

EXECUTIVE FUNCTIONING 7

OUR LIVES: LOOKING DOWN THE ROAD 10

TRASH AS TREASURE 12

ABOUT CLUTTER   13

WHAT I HAD TO WORK WITH 15

STARING AT THE WALLS 15

THE EXTERIOR

GETTING STARTED 20

GETTING THE COLORS RIGHT 23

WHAT TO DO ABOUT THE WALL? 28

THE ROOMS INSIDE

MY GOALS 32

Alone, Together 33

COLLECTING IDEAS 35

Leaving Room to Grow 36

MAKING A SCENE IN THE FOYER 40

THE DEN: CREATING THE PERFECT PLACE FOR PLAY AND WORK 45

Getting Started 45

Choosing the Paint Colors 46

The World Outside 48

Creating Movement and Texture 49

Adding Drama to the Bookshelves 51

A Relaxing Space for Work, Too 55

Making Room for Memories 55

Supporting Small Businesses 57

One Statement Piece on This Mantel. That's It. 58

Sheet Music as Wall Art 61

Bringing It All Together 62

THE ATRIUM 63

Starting with the Walls 66

Stylin' the Mantel 67

The Seating Area 68

Scale: Going Big in a Big Room 69

REIMAGINING THE GUEST BATHROOM 72

TAKING THE STUFFY OUT OF THE LIVING ROOM 76

A New Look 78

The Seating Areas 80

The Sofa: Fixing My Mistake 84

The Lion Chair 87

Mom's Piano 89

REFRESHING THE KITCHEN 92

Looking for Inspiration 92

Giving Myself Elbow Room 94

No Crowds on This Island 98

Pendant Lights for Personality 101

The Breakfast Nook 103

BRINGING THE FOUR-POSTER BEDROOM TO LIFE 105

Balancing the Formal Features with Casual Rugs 105

Artwork That Inspires 107

Curtains: Custom-Made Quality for Half the Price 110

Sleep! 112

Making Room for Exercise 113

THE RIDDLE OF THE FOUR-POSTER BATHROOM 116

The *Cleopatra* Tub Is a Keeper. But the Wallpaper Wants to Stick Around, Too. 117

Removing That Decades-Old Wallpaper 117

Painting the Walls 118

Turning the Jetted Bathtub into a Soaking Tub 119

The Bathroom Is Just the Place for a Washable Rug 121

SOFTENING THE STUDY 124

THE GUESTHOUSE

THE LIVING ROOM: TONING DOWN THE TOILE 130

The Long Search for the Right Rug 133

Going Big with the Mantel 135

THE BEDROOMS 138

The Big Bedroom: Creating a Quiet Space 138

Making the Smaller Bedroom Feel Spacious 145

THE BATHROOM 149

THE GALLEY KITCHEN FINDS ITS GROOVE 150

Replacing the Countertops 150

Looking for Inspiration 154

A Funky Plant as a Focal Point 155

Welcoming Guests 159

AFTERWORD 160

INDEX 164

PREFACE

After I finished writing this book and sent the draft to my editor, I dared myself to give the type of design I describe here a name. I decided to call it Benessent Design after the Latin phrase for well-being, *bene essere*. Naming something that had no name might seem presumptuous. It feels presumptuous. But I feel so strongly about the benefits of addressing design from this perspective that I'll name it to give it a place in our language and in our awareness.

Benessent Design, as I envision it, is about designing spaces to support the emotional and intellectual needs of real people, so they have what they need to thrive as whole human beings. For centuries, rooms and furnishings have been designed to support people's physical needs. Wingback chairs, for example, helped contain heat from a fireplace and shield sitters from drafts so they could stay warm.[1] Canopy beds provided warmth and privacy to a house's lord and lady back in the days when their attendants and servants slept in the same bedroom.[2]

Now, when most of our physical needs have been met through central heating, indoor plumbing, electricity, and refrigeration—and we realize the destructive and often multigenerational consequences of poor mental health—we're becoming more aware of the needs of our minds and less shy about discussing them. Today, we know an enriched environment that includes social support, regular aerobic exercise, good nutrition, and high-quality sleep helps protect our minds against anxiety and depression. These four pillars also support our executive functioning, so we can focus, plan and organize, regulate our emotions, and create.

---

1 "History of Wing Chairs," HomeThingsPast, https://homethingspast.com/2011/12/28/history-wing-chairs/

2 "The Unexpected Original Use of the Canopy Bed," Hunker https://www.hunker.com/13726027/history-of-canopy-bed/

All four are also crucial to keeping our brains healthy for life. Such an enriched environment helps our brains continue to grow and develop, even as we age. Creating this lifelong capacity is a crucial area of study as our population grows older. It's also encouraging news: we can take steps now to help us stay "sharp as a tack" and age happily in place.

Benessent Design honors two design approaches that have been celebrated for years: *wabi-sabi*,[3] the centuries-old Japanese aesthetic concept that finds beauty in imperfection, impermanence, and simplicity; and *hygge*,[4] the Danish cultural emphasis on choices in daily life that bring quiet comfort.

But Benessent Design goes further in its deliberate focus on promoting all aspects of mental health from an evidence-based perspective, as well as from empirical and artistic ones—as it fosters executive functioning; feelings of comfort and safety; intellectual and creative stimulation; and lifelong brain health through good nutrition, regular exercise, sleep, and an enriched environment.

Benessent Design treats our mental health needs as no less important than the needs of the rest of our bodies. Such an approach may even lead us to become better—more creative, more focused, and more productive—and help our brains continue to develop over our lifetimes.

In *Design for Your Mind*, I show how I approached these mental health goals in the house I renovated, and I hope it fires ideas for your own home. Above all, I hope this book leaves you with a lens through which you can view design—a tool that's most valuable when it helps us thrive as whole people and as individuals. Make room for your brilliant life.

---

3 "Wabi Sabi Style: A Guide to Unconventional Interior Design," *Robern*

4 What Is Hygge?, *The Spruce*

MY PARENTS LEFT THEIR HOUSE TO ME. I DECIDED TO REIMAGINE IT IN WAYS THAT WOULD HELP ME REMEMBER THE WHOLE OF MY PARENTS' LIVES—NOT JUST THOSE SAD FINAL YEARS—AS I REBUILT MY OWN LIFE. THE PROCESS HAS HELPED ME WORK THROUGH MY GRIEF OVER MY PARENTS' FINAL STRUGGLES AND APPRECIATE THE FULLNESS OF THEIR LIVES. IT HAS ALSO HELPED ME TAKE STOCK OF MY OWN LIFE AND FIND MY WAY FORWARD.

Introduction

WHY DESIGN?

I have a personal stake in design. During my parents' final years, my father fought a fierce battle with Parkinson's. Meanwhile, my mother—a brilliant, self-taught pianist—was drifting away. Mom had spent years in a wheelchair, and now her mind was fading. I am their oldest child, and a daughter, and I lived in the house next door.

During the years of Dad's 3 a.m., insomnia-fueled phone calls (his wee-hours call list included the bishop and the local police), nights in the emergency room (often after a fall when Mom or Dad had been doing something they had promised not to do), and weeks of visits to rehab (the consequence of said falls), I began to lose myself. Between my parents' health and my job, I had little space to think beyond my immediate responsibilities and little time or energy to maintain my home or my relationships with the outside world—or even with myself.

My siblings and I would spend hours in conference calls, discussing our parents' current conditions and brainstorming about how we might persuade them to accept the help of a paid caregiver, even for a few hours a week. We would cheer when they relented, only to learn our parents had fired the new caregiver within a couple of days. Mom and Dad felt affronted by advice from their children, so as their conditions advanced, any protection we provided—even to members of the driving public and pedestrians—was choreographed after exhaustive sibling discussions.

Those years have left me feeling a bond with other family caregivers and an understanding of the costs and rewards of this journey. In my case, the rewards were abundant. When my parents finally stopped driving, I would take them to church on Saturday evenings. We'd have dinners during the week—often at Subway. I would fetch our tuna melts, and we'd eat them in the car as we watched the trains go by.

INTRODUCTION

When Dad progressed to using a feeding tube—because Parkinson's, with its implacable indifference, continued to come back for more—my parents and I would camp out on their huge bed and talk. That is, until Parkinson's took Dad's voice.

I knew those times would never come again, and I also knew sharing those times with them was a gift. I surprised myself with a new patience I'd thought was beyond my reach, and I realized that joy and sadness can live together in the same heart. I hope this book speaks to people who are dealing with similar challenges and rewards. And I hope, as we come through this experience, we know we're enriched by it and not diminished.

If you're an empty nester; newly widowed, divorced, or single; a young adult moving into your first apartment; or anyone else making a new beginning, this book is for you, too. We can all create spaces that express and empower and support us as we move ahead.

Dad's mind remained clear until two weeks before he died. He'd been a hard-charging captain of industry, a risk-taker, and a dynamic leader. My siblings and I would sit beside him as he lay in bed and talk with him about work. Until Parkinson's stole his voice, Dad would still give us advice.

Then, early one morning, unbeknownst to the caregiver on duty (and for reasons we still don't understand), Dad went down to the basement. We suspect he was feeling in the dark for a light switch when he fell. The paramedics came, and we lost him ten days later.

Over the next four years, Mom's light continued to dim. My brothers would drive from out of state to be with her. And, when it came time for hospice care at home, my sister and I would sit by Mom's bed in shifts. We were grateful she never forgot our names or failed to recognize us. She told us often that she loved us, even if, in her final days, only with the touch of her hand. She was our mom to the end.

After Mom died, my sister and I spent more than a year sorting through our parents' belongings and arranging for their distribution while the estate went through probate.

My parents left their house to me. I decided to reimagine it in ways that would help me remember the whole of my parents' lives—not just those sad final years—as I rebuilt my own life. The process has helped me work through my grief over my parents' final struggles and appreciate the fullness of their lives. It has also helped me take stock of my own life and find my way forward.

A ROOM OF ONE'S OWN

Since I was a child, I've had a passion for creating spaces that are both beautiful and livable: spaces that stimulate and inspire, soothe and welcome. I started with my half of the bedroom that my sister and I shared.

One day, when Mom came home from the thrift store with an old privacy screen, a new age dawned. My sister and I would have our own rooms—one-half each of the bedroom that we shared.

One side held the closet, and the other side the door. After two rounds of Rock Paper Scissors and some tears, we negotiated the precise footpath that the interloper would be permitted to travel to and from the door or the closet. The result was a milestone: each of us had a space to call our own. To arrange and decorate and fuss over. To take pride in.

For me, the room was an oasis of privacy, a refuge where I could think and read and write. During our mandated afternoon naps, I wrote and illustrated my first book. It was called *Lost*, about a girl who is shipwrecked on an island and survives by making friends with the animals. On the other side of the screen, my sister would count the pennies in her piggy bank.

WHY WE NEED PERSONAL SPACE

I also have a professional stake in design. I'm a mental health therapist. I know that healthy mental functioning requires space to think one's own thoughts and express them and build

Photo 2. Here, my sister and I share a bike— more happily than we shared a bedroom.

a relationship with oneself. In childhood and adolescence, the essential developmental tasks are to build autonomy (or the experience of oneself as separate from one's primary caregiver) and self-efficacy (or confidence in one's ability to exert control over one's own motivation, behavior, and social environment).[5]

These are the fundamental building blocks of a healthy personality. They're essential to resilience, focus, critical thinking, healthy relationships, emotional regulation, self-discipline, problem-solving, creativity, a sense of mastery—in short, everything that equips us to handle life's challenges and thrive.

5 A. Bandura, "Self-Efficacy: Toward a Unifying Theory of Behavioral Change," *Psychol Rev.* 84 (1977): 191–215, doi: 10.1037/0033-295X.84.2.191.

PERSONAL SPACE IN AN ENMESHED FAMILY

Personal space is especially important in families who are enmeshed because, in an enmeshed family, no boundaries separate family members. Instead, the members are fused together by unhealthy emotions, often anxiety, that can be rooted in trauma or illness.[6] Parents might discourage boundaries because they rely on a child for emotional support and feel threatened by the child's growing independence. Parents might fear being abandoned and may smother the child's sense of self by meddling in personal decisions and/or undermining the child's confidence with belittling, bullying, shunning, scapegoating, or other forms of abuse. But all members of an enmeshed family need personal space to develop as individuals and exercise autonomy in their own lives.[7] If they don't find that space at home, it's common for one or more members of an enmeshed family to cut ties upon reaching adulthood and become estranged. That's generally a last-ditch effort to achieve autonomy.

6   "Enmeshment: Definition, Relationship Signs, Finding Balance," *Verywell Health*, https://www.verywellhealth.com/enmeshment-healing-steps-5223635

7   "The Enmeshed Family System: What It Is and How to Break Free," *Psych Central*, https://psychcentral.com/blog/imperfect/2019/05/the-enmeshed-family-system-what-it-is-and-how-to-break-free

WE ALSO NEED ONE ANOTHER

At the same time, we all need social support—the acceptance, encouragement, stimulation, and learning that we give to others and others give to us. We need safe spaces, and we need the confidence to leave our safe spaces to take risks, to have adventures. We need social support to learn the skills to communicate in constructive ways, however imperfect our efforts might be. That's how we grow.

Designing spaces that foster our mental health has become more important as many of us work from home. And it can be even more important for young people who lack the ability to roam alone and explore the world outside that many of us enjoyed growing up, or who may not be able to leave home. Designing one's space can offer an additional freedom: one can take risks without threatening one's safety. And one can exercise agency: we design the set and direct the production.

Psychologists speak of the *locus of control*. It's the degree to which people believe that they, as opposed to external forces beyond their influence, control the outcomes of events in their lives.[8] The theory holds that our sense of well-being is tied to the degree to which we believe we have control over our lives and our environments. The more remote that control is from us, the more distressed we feel.

If your experience as a caregiver or your experience in another role involved loss of control over your privacy, time, decision-making, and sense of well-being, you can take steps to reclaim it. I hope you find that expressing yourself through interior design helps you discover your power, explore your creativity, and strengthen your voice. I hope you can hear your own voice and believe in it. And I hope you love creating spaces that support and stimulate you as you move forward into the rest of your life.

EXECUTIVE FUNCTIONING

I was cleaning out a closet in the house during the renovation when I discovered some of my grade-school report cards my mom had stashed away. The teachers' comments reacquainted me with a child who devoured books with joy, but who nonetheless left authority

---

[8] Julian B. Rotter, "Generalized Expectancies for Internal versus External Control of Reinforcement," *Psychological Monographs: General and Applied*, 80, no. 1 (1966): 1–28, doi:10.1037/h0092976, PMID 5340840, S2CID 15355866.

figures disgruntled. I was polite and well-behaved, they said, but I daydreamed in class, and sometimes, I'd have to stay after school to complete classroom assignments.

I was too ashamed to tell my parents why I daydreamed. I'd become discouraged because teachers sometimes frowned when I put my hand up in class. "Let's hear from somebody else," they'd say, and I'd interpreted their response as a scolding, a message that I had done something wrong. Over time, I disengaged. I let my mind leave the classroom and go elsewhere. I had no reason to plan and organize, and I even cultivated a sweater-losing forgetfulness, making me a problem of another sort.

After a couple of years, my parents moved my sister and me to another school, where I fell in love with every class. I was motivated to plan and organize because I found my classes exciting, and I knew planning and organizing was key to doing well in them. Mrs. Salvati's English class was heaven. She would assign a creative writing topic and then give us forty-five minutes to write an essay. We would turn in the finished work at the end of class, and the following week, she would choose one of us to read our essay to the class.

All this came back to me as I went through the records my mom had kept. I wished my parents were still with me, so I could talk with them. Their decision to move my sister and me to the new school changed our lives. As a grown-up, I understood that it had been a big financial commitment, and I wished I could thank them in person.

The planning and organizing I practiced in that classroom are part of our executive functioning skills. Also included are the skills we use to solve problems, schedule appointments, finish assignments, and meet deadlines. And we use our executive functioning to keep track of ideas when we create. These skills are the scaffolding that supports our other abilities, and we depend on them to function effectively in the world. They provide us with structure. We can think of them as the table of contents or the index in our mammoth mental reference book. Executive functioning skills make our thoughts easier to navigate and manage, and we spend our lives refining them.

INTRODUCTION

Our executive functioning skills also help us regulate our emotions and control our impulses. So, when our executive functioning is impaired—because of stress, lack of sleep, distractions, or anything else—we're more likely to forget to pay our bills on time, lose our tax paperwork, show up late, and otherwise let ourselves and others down. It's not a fun way to live.

For people who live with attention deficit hyperactivity disorder (ADHD), executive functioning is a particular challenge. That's because, with ADHD, the prefrontal cortex (the part of the brain responsible for executive functioning) needs extra support.[9]

Specialized advice for designing spaces for people living with attention deficit hyperactivity disorder, autism spectrum disorder (ASD), or sensory processing disorder is beyond the scope of this book. But, in general, tools we can use to moderate stimulation include weighted blankets, dimmer switches on lights, window shades and curtains, music, muted colors, and soft textures. A low clutter, well-ordered environment supports executive functioning and helps prevent overstimulation. Aim to designate specific places in your home for specific tasks, and to ban from the bedroom online activities that might interfere with sleep.[10]

Executive functioning can also be a challenge for neurotypical people who are inclined to ponder, and for lots of other people. Designing a space that supports our executive functioning can make a big difference to our productivity and our sense of well-being and confidence. Throughout this book, we'll talk about ways to do that.

---

9   "The Emerging Neurobiology of Attention Deficit Hyperactivity Disorder: The Key Role of the Prefrontal Association Cortex," *Pub Med Central*

10 "What is Executive Dysfunction and How You Can Manage It," Henry Ford Health – Detroit, MI

INTRODUCTION

OUR LIVES: LOOKING DOWN THE ROAD

Designing our homes to support our mental health now is only part of the story. We can also take steps to help our brains remain healthy in the future. Studies suggest that the same choices we make to enhance focus, productivity, and mental equilibrium today can slow or prevent our cognitive decline over the years to come.

As our population ages, scientists are exploring ways to design environments to help prevent memory loss and other changes associated with our older years. The COVID-19 pandemic also spurred interest in this inquiry. The lockdown brought extreme and extended social isolation that affected the mental health of people young, old, and in-between.

Many of these people were residents of senior living facilities who had been diagnosed with Alzheimer's disease and other forms of dementia. Loss of face-to-face contact with their loved ones and other normal social stimulation deepened their loneliness and, in many cases, accelerated their mental deterioration and physical decline.[11] COVID-19 was a tragedy of human suffering, and the consequences of the lockdown drove home the crucial importance of social support and an enriched environment, not only for people experiencing cognitive decline, but for those who choose to work to prevent or mitigate it.

The human brain has a trait called neuroplasticity. That's the brain's ability to change its function and structure in response to our experiences.[12] We associate this ability with children as we watch them absorb new information and acquire new skills at an accelerated pace. But, in fact, our brains retain much of their neuroplasticity throughout our lives.

---

11 "The Sars-Cov-2 Pandemic and the Brave New Digital World of Environmental Enrichment to Prevent Brain Aging and Cognitive Decline," *The Journal of Prevention of Alzheimer's Disease*

12 "Enriched Environments for Brain Health that Foster Creativity, Promote Positivity, and Reduce Stress: A Neurogenesis Hypothesis," *HKS Architects*, https://www.hksinc.com/how-we-think/reports/enriched-environments-for-brain-health-that-foster-creativity-promote-positivity-and-reduce-stress-a-neurogenesis-hypothesis/

INTRODUCTION

Not only can we keep our brains stimulated during adulthood to keep our mental functioning sharp,[13] but we can also develop and strengthen our brains. Writing stories, taking up a new musical instrument, learning to play chess, and learning a new language are among the activities that increase our brains' neuroplasticity.[14] These activities build our brains' cerebral reserve, or resilience capacity, that helps our brains remain functional as we grow older.[15]

Throughout this book, we'll discuss design choices that can benefit us now and also keep our brains healthy over the years.

But we can summarize those long-term benefits here. Our brains are helped by:
- Enriching our environments with colors, textures, and shapes[16]
- Kindling our memories with furniture, photos, or recipes passed down by loved ones
- Surrounding ourselves with art, music, and nature
- Designing our spaces so we can get together with friends on short notice, making social connections easier and bringing us its stress-buffering benefits[17]
- Designing our spaces so we can create music, write stories, and paint, providing us with stimulation, novelty, and cognitive challenge
- Designing our bedrooms to make sure we get good-quality sleep that promotes our ability to process learning and memory and restore our brains' plasticity[18]

---

13 "Architecture for Preventing Cognitive Decline: Contributions from Neuroscience to Healthy Aging," ArchDaily, https://www.archdaily.com/1007274/architecture-for-preventing-cognitive-decline-contributions-from-neuroscience-to-healthy-aging

14 "The Combined Influences of Exercise, Diet and Sleep on Neuroplasticity," Frontiers

15 "Healthy Lifestyle and Cognition in Older Adults with Common Neuropathologies of Dementia," JAMA Network

16 "Environmental Factors Promoting Neural Plasticity: Insights from Animal and Human Studies," PubMed Central

17 "Neurobiology of Loneliness, Isolation, and Loss: Integrating Human and Animal Perspectives," Frontiers

18 "Sleep On It," NIH News in Health

- Setting up an area in our houses where we can exercise, regardless of weather conditions or time of day, to encourage aerobic exercise for reasons that include increasing blood flow to our brains[19]
- Setting up our kitchens to make cooking healthy meals easy and fun, and protecting our brains with foods that reduce oxidative stress and inflammation[20]

The design choices we make today deliver returns today. But they're also investments in our healthy mental functioning for the rest of our lives.

TRASH AS TREASURE

When my sister and I were little, Mom gave us chores. My favorite was emptying the wastebaskets. I would stand at the trash cans and go through the contents of every wastebasket, fishing out things I thought could be salvaged and repurposed for something else. I'd come back to the house with old lampshades, empty thread spools, pieces of fabric, an empty cardboard toilet paper roll—anything I thought deserved another chance. Mom threw up her hands and gave wastebasket-emptying duties to my sister.

Decades later, I still see throwaway stuff as material for something else. And I save things—old letters, books, cards—anything that preserves a record or a memory. So as I planned to renovate the house, I knew I'd find a way to repurpose, upcycle, donate, or recycle everything deemed unwanted. As we go along, I will let you know the uses I found for discarded items, and maybe you can find homes for some of your own.

Seeing the value in these things and giving them new life—as I worked to give new life to the house and to myself—was part of the joy of the renovation.

---

19 Ibid., 9.
20 See, for example: https://nutritionsource.hsph.harvard.edu/healthy-weight/diet-reviews/mind-diet/

INTRODUCTION

ABOUT CLUTTER

As you may guess, my "saving" tendencies tee me right up for a tendency to accumulate clutter. And clutter is a big deal. In recent years, clutter has been the subject of research that explores its impacts on executive functioning and decision-making, stress levels, self-esteem, energy, overeating, and other behaviors related to our mental and physical health. Research suggests that when our environments are cluttered, our ability to focus is restricted because every item in our cluttered environment is competing for our attention. As a result, we're distracted, and being distracted limits our brains' ability to process information. We focus on tasks better in an uncluttered and organized environment. And our executive functioning skills perform better.

Because controlling clutter is so important to our mental health and to our quality of life, I'll provide links to a few articles on the subject in the footnotes. I like to understand the "whys" of human and animal behavior, and I'm guessing you do, too. I zeroed in on articles that broaden our understanding of the effects of clutter on our brains and don't insult our intelligence by stating and restating the obvious.

Reducing clutter doesn't always mean getting rid of things. Some articles offer tips as simple as setting up easy and attractive ways to store items so they no longer bombard your senses and create visual chaos when you walk into a room. Others show you how to manage the things you own so you can find them easily and use them right away. It might be as easy as organizing your books by categories so you can find and read the books that interest you. And eliminating clutter doesn't mean making your environment sterile. You can design an environment that holds memories and meaning without creating clutter. You'll find a link below to one of the best articles I have found on the subject.[21]

21 "Massive Psychological Effects of Clutter, According to Science," *Mia Danielle*

TAKING SOME OF THE HEADACHE OUT OF DECLUTTERING

Whether you're cleaning out your parents' house, reorganizing your own house, or finding the floor in the bedroom you grew up in, decluttering is no one's favorite job. The best we can do is make it less overwhelming and help speed the results so we can see them and know we're making real progress. I'll mention resources that helped make the job easier for me as we get to them, but I want to summarize them here to save you time.

- Vietnam Veterans of America (VVA) picked up books, clothing, household items, and small furniture at no charge. I scheduled pickups online and left the boxes and bags on my front porch.[22]
- I posted items on the local "Buy Nothing" page on Facebook and—to ensure my safety and give the person receiving the items peace of mind—made the transfers in the parking lot of a local supermarket.
- My local library and the school in my neighborhood collected my used books for their annual book sales.
- Unexpired and unopened medical supplies and medical equipment went to a nonprofit that ships the items to its missions abroad.
- Furniture the auctioneer had rejected went to an organization that gives vouchers to families to be redeemed for free household goods at its warehouse. (The auctioneer had rejected all upholstered furniture, regardless of its condition. He'd explained that large items of upholstered furniture are difficult to sell at auction.)
- Clothing and household items in excellent condition could have been resold on eBay and Poshmark.
- High-quality furniture could have been resold on AptDeco.

I rented a dumpster to discard items that no one wanted.

22 "About VVA," *Pickup Please, https://pickupplease.org/about-vva*

INTRODUCTION

WHAT I HAD TO WORK WITH

The outside of the house and every room inside needed work, and I knew costs could spin out of control if I didn't have a plan. I used the free technology that's widely available to hatch ideas for modestly priced changes that would have a big impact. I auditioned paint colors for free on the Benjamin Moore website, and I collected ideas on Pinterest (also free). I ordered many of the goods online through Etsy, eBay, AptDeco, Poshmark, and other affordable outlets. I also found some cool things in thrift stores and tackled some DIY projects.

STARING AT THE WALLS

But my most valuable resource—also free—is my imagination, as it is yours. I would sit and stare at a space, or at a photo of a space, and think about how I wanted to use the room and how I wanted to feel when I walked into it. In time, I saw shapes, colors, and textures in the space. Then I thought about what I could use in that space that I already had, could make, or could find on Etsy or eBay that held the shape, color, or texture I envisioned.

I thought about how the eye moves through a space, and I designed each room to direct that movement. I combined stimulation with comfort. Stimulation might spring from a surprising piece of sculpture or other art, or a "warm" color like red. Comfort might come from the soothing textures of a throw pillow or rug; "cool" blues with greens, and plants, neutral colors, glass, stone, wood, and other natural materials.[23] I combined family antiques with modern furniture and other modern elements, so neither my guests nor I would feel stuck in an era.

---

23 "Warm" colors are reds, oranges, and yellows. "Cool" colors are blues, greens, and purples. When we get to the smaller bedroom in the guesthouse, we'll discuss how painting a room with a warm or a cool color can make the room feel smaller or larger.

INTRODUCTION

This book will take you, room by room, through the renovations I made, but my overall approach was not one room at a time. I directed my physical labor to one room at a time, but I would also be firing up ideas for others. I used a notebook to keep track of the paint colors I was considering, and I created separate boards on Pinterest for each room and would capture ideas as they came to me. Ideas would announce themselves in my sleep, on a walk, and at other times when I wasn't aware I had been thinking about a design challenge. I kept all these ideas organized, so I could come back to them when I was ready to start my physical work on a particular room.

Pursuing a creative challenge in this nonlinear fashion has its advantages. First, your imagination has a mind of its own. It doesn't care if you're carrying groceries to your car, working out at the gym, or doing laundry. Once you give your imagination an assignment, it will get to work and come back to you with solutions, even when you don't have a free hand to write them down.

But your imagination needs time to come up with the best solutions. Posing challenges to it from the beginning will spare you the stress of starting with a blank slate when you turn your attention to the next room. The nonlinear approach might also fuel the best solutions because you can give every solution you consider ample time to germinate. You'll develop your ideas and improve on them every time you think about them.[24]

When we think creatively, multiple regions of our brains are coordinating their work: our executive control network handles the planning, organizing, problem-solving, and decision-making. Our default-mode network is activated, looking for ideas as we let our minds wander. Our salience network is sensitive to the feelings we associate with rewards, such as knowing that we have created something inspiring or soothing or well-organized. All this busyness is going on as our brains generate possible solutions to each creative challenge (known as divergent thinking) and zero in on a final solution to the problem (known as

---

24   "Creativity and the Brain" *Psychology Today*

convergent thinking). Other regions of our brains are involved in creativity, but basically, our brains are having a blast. Working on design challenges is exuberant mental exercise.[25]

A word about stress. Reimagining spaces in your home is a gift you give yourself and your loved ones. You're doing this to create a home that helps take care of you. So I hope you let this work be fun and not a headache. The process is a big part of the gift, and you'll learn a lot about your eye and the way you approach challenges and create. When you encounter delays and frustrations, you can jump to plans for another room, whether it's exploring paint colors or looking for new dish towels online. There's always something you can do to move forward.

Another thing: our houses will never be "done." Don't wait until yours is a finished masterpiece to invite your friends over and have fun in it. If your friends are like my friends and me, we love seeing works in progress and cheering one another's hard work and ingenuity.

This is your home. If you stay playful and see the beauty in its progress, I think you'll be happier with the results.

25   Ibid., 2, 5.

I WANTED TO UNCOVER THE HOUSE'S BEAUTY, DUST IT OFF, AND MAYBE REINTERPRET IT. I WANTED TO BRING THE HOUSE ALIVE.

The Exterior

Photo 3. The house, "before." The elegant transom over the front door adds still more straight lines to the façade.

GETTING STARTED

I was not burning to turn the house my parents had left me into something other than what it was. I had no ambition to tear down walls or gut any part of it. No matter my budget, I did not want to erase traces of my parents or our family's time together.

I wanted to uncover the house's beauty, dust it off, and maybe reinterpret it. I wanted to bring the house alive.

THE EXTERIOR

Photo 4. The house, "before." The triangular area inside the top of the portico is painted white. That makes the white portico look even bigger.

But first I needed to understand it. I used to sit on the wall outside and study it, guessing at its architectural style. I would also try to figure out what worked for the house and what didn't, as I tried to grasp what the house was and what it needed from me.

I took photos and uploaded them to the Benjamin Moore website so I could experiment with paint colors.[26] In this chapter, you'll find a few of the "before" photos. Let's start with Photo 3. If you look around Mom's wheelchair van, you'll find a one-story house with huge, square columns beneath a massive portico. You may notice that the portico and columns are out of scale with the rest of the house. They dominate the eye, and you don't see much else.

26 Benjamin Moore paints and stains, https://www.benjaminmoore.com/

Photo 5. The wall, "before." At least the urn was safe.

The house is a study in straight lines and sharp angles, right down to the two huge, square planter boxes that the former owners installed on either side of the front door. Those boxes are adorned with a crisscross design, adding more straight lines and sharp angles.

The color is a cold, pale gray. The shutters are white. Because there's little contrast between the colors of the shutters and the exterior walls, the eye is not invited to travel along the breadth of the house. Instead, it is trapped by the outsized columns and the portico.

And the eye doesn't draw comfort or a sense of welcome or warmth from the collection of straight lines and sharp angles that congregate at the front door. Notice that in Photo 4, even the boxwood shrubs that stand at attention in front of the big windows have been clipped in a harsh buzz cut, like fresh recruits at a boot camp. The house is begging for softness and fun.

In Photo 5, you'll see that surrounding the roundabout driveway is a brick wall that was painted the same pale gray as the house. Two massive concrete urns are mounted on each front pillar where the wall separates to admit visitors. Every summer, the urns would sprout tufts of crabgrass or whatever else the birds had dropped into them.

After my dad mis-steered a few times when driving up to the house, he had two red-and-white safety poles installed at each pillar to protect the wall. The result looked like the whimsical drop-off entrance to an emergency room. Even after Dad stopped driving, the poles remained, although the paramedics did not need them as guideposts when they visited.

GETTING THE COLORS RIGHT

I found a company called Samplize that sells large peel-and-stick samples of paint colors from Benjamin Moore, Sherwin-Williams, Farrow & Ball, and PPG Paints.[27] What a step up from those messy little cans of sample colors we used to buy at the paint store!

I guessed that the house's architectural style is modern Greek Revival, judging from its large portico and columns, the symmetry of its design, and its details, including the entrance marked by sidelights and a rectangular transom. It's unusual to see a one-story house with this architectural style, and I still hadn't solved the mystery of that out-of-scale portico and imposing columns.

A little research online showed me that the traditional colors for a Greek Revival house, modern or not, are an off-white or yellow body with white trim and dark shutters. I wanted to stay true to the architectural style, but another advantage of this color combination was that it would provide the contrast necessary to unlock the eye from the portico and

---

27 Paint samples by Samplize, https://samplize.com/

columns and invite it to travel to the dark shutters and along the breadth of the house. That way, the eye can appreciate the house's symmetry.

Researchers have explored the effects of symmetry in art and nature on the human brain. As it turns out, people like it. Symmetry is easy for our brains to process, and we are attracted to the order it represents.[28] In addition to Greek Revival, think of Georgian architecture and the classical architecture of Greece and Rome that influenced the later styles. All of them are characterized by symmetry in placement of doors, windows, columns, porticoes, and other details.

So, for the body of the house, I hunted for off-white colors with a hint of yellow and loaded the Benjamin Moore website with mock-ups in different tints of off-white.[29] After I narrowed the field to my three finalists, I emailed the mock-ups to my friend Catherine, whose eye I trust, and I asked for her thoughts. She picked Blossom Tint as the winner, and I thank her for that. It's an off-white that lifts the spirits but isn't sentimental in any light.

The shutters had to be dark enough to provide a sharp contrast to the body of the house, but I wanted the overall effect to be soft and welcoming, not harsh. So I steered away from black. I was also wary of any navy that can lean toward bright blue when the sun shines on it.

The trick was to find a navy that was *almost* black, but not quite. Voilà! Here's French Beret by Benjamin Moore. It's a navy *tone*—that is, navy with the addition of gray and not black. French Beret is dark enough to never lean blue, but *not-black* enough to be soft and mysterious.[30]

28 "Why Do We Get So Much Pleasure From Symmetry?" *HowStuffWorks*

29 "Hue, Tint, Tone, and Shade: What's the Difference?" *Color Wheel Artist*

30 Benjamin Moore French Beret has an LRV (light reflectance value) of 9.06 out of 100. That's very low. Generally, a dark blue exterior will appear bluer when hit with direct sunlight and will almost appear like navy black when not in the sun. The very low LRV of French Beret means that, even when direct sunlight hits it, it will not appear blue. That's because a color with a very low LRV will absorb almost all light and reflect very little.

THE EXTERIOR

Photo 6. The house, "after." To soften the look of the portico, I chose the Blossom Tint color you see on the body of the house for the inside triangle of the portico. The Simply White trim color in that area would have made the portico look even larger.

Body: Blossom Tint by Benjamin Moore
Trim: Simply White by Benjamin Moore
Shutters: French Beret by Benjamin Moore

For the trim, I chose Benjamin Moore's Simply White. It's a warm off-white with a hint of yellow that does not cast a yellow tint in any light. It's warm enough not to be stark or cold, but not too warm to contrast with the warm Blossom Tint body of the house. I chose that trim color for the columns, the frame of the portico, the window frames, and the fascia that separates the roof from the body of the house. Photo 6 shows the result with the final colors.

Photo 7. The house, "after." I planted poplars in the urns to add more softness to the entrance with greenery and a disciplined but graceful shape.

What about those massive concrete urns? In my mission to soften the look of the house, I moved them from atop the pillars and set them on either side of the front door, replacing the straight lines of the planter boxes with the curved lines of the urns.

THE EXTERIOR

Photo 8. The house, "after." The urns have found their best place, and they won't be sprouting crabgrass in the summer anymore.

THE EXTERIOR

Photo 9. The wall, "after." We plan to give the wall a light coating with a product called Classico Limewash by Romabio. Unlike most paint products, limewash is formulated to allow bricks to "breathe," so they don't trap moisture and crumble. I chose solid concrete artichokes on pedestals because they're not pillar ornaments one sees every day. And, unlike a planter that can sprout weeds or a light fixture that might malfunction, they require no maintenance.

Romabio, Classico Limewash
"Pineapple" finials by CementBarn (etsy.com)
Concrete urn plinth pedestal by Compania International

WHAT TO DO ABOUT THE WALL?

I couldn't think of a paint color for the pale-gray brick wall that surrounded the driveway roundabout that wouldn't distract from the fresh look of the newly painted house. It finally dawned on me that I could strip the paint and let the bricks go naked.

Problem was, no contractor or painter I spoke with wanted the job. It was too big, they said. The job would be so time-consuming and labor-intensive that the cost would be prohibitive.

So, with his typical resourcefulness, Kurt did it himself. I found a DIY paint-stripping product called Smart Strip Advanced Paint Remover by Dumond. It's environmentally friendly and nontoxic, with no hazardous fumes and no odor, and it works with sheets of laminated paper that we purchased separately. The laminated paper keeps the paint remover in a wet state so it can do its work over a couple of days. With a power sander, paint scraper, and the paint remover, Kurt tackled the wall.

He's not quite finished, but we like to think of it as a labor of love. Photo 9 shows the wall now.

I HOPE YOU LEAVE YOURSELF ROOM TO GROW IN YOUR DESIGN CHOICES BECAUSE YOU MAY GROW IN WAYS THAT SURPRISE YOU. I HOPE YOU MAKE CHOICES THAT WOULD WORK WELL IN ANOTHER ROOM, OR THAT COULD BE REIMAGINED WITHOUT UNDUE EXPENSE OR EFFORT, AS YOUR VOICE BECOMES STRONGER AND YOUR EYE BECOMES MORE DISCERNING.

The Rooms Inside

MY GOALS

Next, I turned to the rooms inside the house. After years of struggling to keep up with housework and stay in contact with friends as I juggled my responsibilities to my parents with my job as a therapist, I craved order, peace of mind, and a sense of control.

I wanted my new house to be well-organized, well-maintained, and uncluttered, with everything in its place. I wanted to feel uplifted and inspired as I walked through the rooms, not frustrated and overwhelmed.[31] And I wanted to create a place where I could welcome friends and other guests for parties, cooking classes, overnight visits, hanging out, listening to music, or watching movies.

The pandemic struck during the last year and a half of my mom's life. To this day, we are thankful we were able to keep her safe from infection and only vaguely aware that something had shaken the world outside. But my clients felt the impact of isolation from their peers, and so did I. We all did.[32]

We humans are wired to need social connection, and studies show that when our social needs are not met, we experience a stress response that can trigger anxiety and depression and lead to physical illness.[33] So it's not surprising that reports of anxiety and depression have surged since the beginning of the pandemic. These conditions were likely worsened by the loss of social support as people were confined to their homes or to their care facilities.[34]

---

31   "Why Decluttering Your Home Gives Your Brain An Instant Therapeutic Boost," *Forbes*
32   "Social Isolation Is Worse than Loneliness," *Psychology Today*
33   "The Loneliness Epidemic: Escape Post-pandemic Social Isolation," UC Health
34   Ibid.

When we resurfaced, I'd had enough of Zoom calls and social distancing. My gold standard became IRL.[35] As much as I treasure my solitude and space, I also need to be with people, to see their faces, hear their voices, laugh with them in person, and enjoy life as part of a community.[36]

ALONE, TOGETHER

Our need for social connection persists, even when we're enjoying our solitude.[37] We take comfort in knowing we're part of a larger whole—that we're not isolated, even when we're alone. We can look through our window at the birds feasting at the feeder and know we're connected to all species through our mutual aliveness, our appetites, and our capacity to feel.

We can look at the table our grandmother inherited from her parents, or whip up biscuits using a recipe passed down through three generations, and we know we're connected to people who have gone before us through our memories and our shared family history.

We can look at a painting or read a work of literature and know we're connected to people we've never met through a shared passion for art and language. Our old yearbooks and photos connect us to our past and the people who helped shape us.

---

35 IRL (in real life) is an abbreviation used to indicate that a person is speaking about something real and outside the digital world of communication, gaming, or virtual reality. From https://www.techtarget.com/

36 There's a difference between being alone (an objective state) and being lonely. Loneliness is the subjective experience of not having one's social needs met, and it can be experienced in a group of friends or in a family. Research suggests that loneliness triggers certain physiological changes that pose risks to mental and physical health, and that its effects can be prevented—and often treated— with changes in lifestyle. My goals for the house, then, included redesigning it to optimize meaningful social connection to maintain my own mental and physical health and the health of those I care about, and to help prevent loneliness in the coming years. See "The Complexity of Loneliness," PMC

37 "Your Brain Is Changed by Social Isolation," *Psychology Today*

BALANCING OUR NEEDS FOR STIMULATION AND SAFETY

I have a guiding principle. It underlies my work as a therapist and my design of these rooms, and it shapes how I've learned to structure my life: all of us need both stimulation and safety. We need both elements in different measures, depending on our stage of life, our appetites, and what we're dealing with on a given day, but both elements must be present in our environment. Too much stimulation without a feeling of safety, and we're rattled and, over time, exhausted. Too much safety without stimulation, and we're bored and agitated. Either imbalance can lead to depression.

Our animals need a balance of stimulation and safety, too. That's why we take our dogs for walks and give them toys and play with them, and it's also why we give them a soft bed and cuddles.

We can use that understanding when we design spaces. A room that's bland and predictable might be playing it safe, but it doesn't create a feeling of safety for the person in it. Instead, it bores. It drains energy, deadens inspiration, and foments agitation because it feels like a trap. On the other hand, a room with a cacophony of patterns, colors, and objects may look exciting and designer-ish, but if it registers in the mind as chaos, it might impress, but it doesn't invite.

Designing spaces that allow us to feel those connections supports our well-being. Feeling those connections is an antidote to isolation, even when no other person is physically present.[38]

38   "Nostalgia May Have Bona Fide Benefits in Hard Times, like the Pandemic," *Science News*

COLLECTING IDEAS

Pinterest is a brilliant invention—one of the healthiest and least toxic uses of social media I've found. I used the boards I created for each room in the house to keep track of ideas, and I spent hours on the site exploring the posts of professional designers and regular people for inspiration. I love to see what professional designers do with their own homes because they take the biggest risks and tend to be the most exuberant in their personal spaces. The professional designers I like often use bold, saturated colors on their walls. They explore the power of the unexpected: the outlandish placement or scale; the incongruous choice of fabric, texture, color, shape, furniture, or artwork; and/or the odd combination of elements, textures, and finishes, such as natural wood with industrial metal, rough with smooth, and matte with high gloss. They balance the exciting elements with textures, shapes, and colors that offer comfort.

These are artists with vision, and they have developed their eye, found their voice, and built the skill to pursue their vision with confidence. The work of great designers and other creative professionals, such as Athena Calderone,[39] Bunny Mellon,[40] Leanne Ford,[41] Matthew Harris,[42] Antony Todd,[43] Monica Calderon and Ezequiel Farca,[44] Hugues Magen,[45] Claire

---

39   Athena Calderone, *Live Beautiful* (New York: Abrams, 2020).

40   Linda Jane Holden, Thomas Lloyd, and Bryan Huffman, *Bunny Mellon Style* (Layton, Utah: Gibbs Smith, 2021).

41   Leanne Ford, *The Slow Down: For the Love of Home* (New York: Abrams, 2024).

42   *Elle Décor*, April 2023.

43   Ibid.

44   *Architectural Digest*, December 2022.

45   Ibid.

Tabouret,[46] and Florian Marquardt,[47] gives me a jolt of energy when they welcome me into their spaces. These artists create spaces that make me feel and think and want to be there.

In my own home, because I'm still developing my eye and voice (and the confidence to use them), I'm drawn to bold choices that I can modify or edit as my vision evolves and my voice grows stronger. So maybe no to screaming pink on the atrium walls—as much as walls in that color would captivate me—but a big yes to the same screaming pink on an accent chair in the buttoned-down study, or a large, screaming pink velvet ottoman in the formal living room, or a flash of screaming pink on a painted canvas.

I love to ride toward a destination, but if I'm inspired to take another direction, I'm ready for a change of course.

LEAVING ROOM TO GROW

Writing this book meant reaching deep to describe my experience and understanding. This was not always fun. Sorting through old letters, books, photos, and mementos brought back memories. Sometimes, I would revisit a memory from a new perspective and build a new appreciation. Other times, I found myself feeling sad or unsettled by a recollection that raised more questions. During the last four years of my mom's life, there were still mysteries I'd hoped to explore with her, but it had been too late.

All this thinking and feeling and remembering expanded my perspective. And it expanded me. When I reconnected to my past, including the pieces I did not fully understand, I connected to my whole self. What's more, I finally had the freedom and the life experience to name what I remembered. As I named my memories, I could process them with my

---

46   Ibid.
47   *Elle Décor*, March 2023.

more developed language. And, in using words, I found my voice. As I renovated the house and wrote about it, my voice became stronger.

How does this relate to design? I didn't understand how processing memories had affected me until I found myself going back to a few rooms I thought I had finished. A piece of art I had chosen weeks before no longer spoke to me. I would replace it with something that exerted a more powerful pull on my emotions or said what I wanted to say without apology. In two rooms, the new and more magnetic work was a reproduction of a color-field painting by Mark Rothko, a twentieth-century American abstract expressionist.

I was reminded, once again, why humans need art. We're drawn to immerse ourselves, not only in our own creative processes, but in the creativity of other people. Creativity, whether revealed through painting, sculpture, writing, music, photography, moviemaking, theater, dance, or design, connects us to ourselves and to our common humanity.

And my writing began to shed its diffidence. It took me a while to notice what was happening and to understand why. I returned to sections of this book to explore more of my reasoning and to reveal my left turns and creative struggles. I looked for words and images free from fluff or fat, that cut closer to the bone. And, as *meta* as this sounds, the very house I had renovated to support and encourage my renewal did just that as I wrote about it.

Clearing the clutter and examining and organizing what remained fueled the focus and creativity I needed to make the house and the book more straightforward expressions of myself. The house became my home, in the truest sense. It also showed me the power of Benessent Design because it supported the process of my writing about it.

If you, too, are making a new beginning, I hope you leave yourself room to grow in your design choices because you may grow in ways that surprise you. I hope you make choices that would work well in another room, or that could be reimagined without undue expense or effort, as your voice becomes stronger and your eye becomes more discerning.

STAYING SAFE AT HOME

When I began these renovations, I would have been hard pressed to tell you which major appliances in the house or the guesthouse operated on gas or electricity. Nor could I have pointed to the water heaters and furnaces on the property that use gas. What's worse, I could not have identified the source of a gas leak if one occurred, or known how to shut the gas off. I also could not have told you why older appliances might be more vulnerable to gas leaks. I knew the people to call for answers, but I couldn't have answered those questions myself.

As we design our homes to help take care of us, it's a good time to protect against the invisible threats that our homes can pose to our safety and the safety of our loved ones and neighbors. One risk is combustible gas vapors that might leak from a connection to an appliance, such as a clothes dryer, or from a malfunctioning or improperly installed water heater, furnace, or generator, or even from that nifty gas-operated fireplace in our living room.

Affordable devices are available that read natural gas, carbon monoxide,[48] and radon[49] levels and send an audible alert when they register danger. Some of these devices plug into a wall outlet and are backed up by a lithium battery in case of a power failure. Others send readings and an alert to a smartphone or a virtual assistant device.

The dangers became real to me after I learned of tragedies that had occurred nearby and in other parts of the country because combustible gas had built up in a house. So as I completed renovations, I installed a gas leak and carbon monoxide detector in every room that had a gas appliance. That meant the kitchen and laundry room in the main house and the

---

48 "Carbon Monoxide Poisoning Basics," Center for Disease Control (CDC)

49 "Radon," *World Health Organization*

guesthouse, the basement, the garage, and every room containing a gas-operated fireplace. At the footnote below, you'll get a link to the simple device I chose[50] and experts' tips for identifying a gas or carbon monoxide leak in your house, along with their recommendations for devices that read levels of natural gas, carbon monoxide, and radon.[51]

And don't forget smoke detectors. They don't have to be those annoying little things that scream from the ceiling every time they run through a battery. Smoke detectors can be hardwired, or they can run on a lithium battery that will last for ten years. The trick is to know the difference between a smoke detector that uses photoelectric technology and one that uses ionization. Photoelectric sensors give the earliest alert to smoldering materials, which is how most household fires start. Smoke detectors that use ionization are sensitive to flames. Below is a link to some choices with explanations about how they work.[52]

These devices are affordable and easy to install and use. They're available in brick-and-mortar stores and through online outlets. And they're worth the small investment to help keep ourselves and our loved ones safe and ensure that we can live safely in our houses as we—along with our houses and appliances—grow older.

They're essential for our protection at every stage in life, whether we've owned a home for years or are moving into our first apartment. We can call this "design for our peace of mind."

---

50 Kidde carbon monoxide detector (kidde.com)
51 "What Does a Carbon Monoxide Detector Do and How Does it Work?" *SafeWise*
52 "The 9 Best Smoke Detectors to Protect Your Home," *Popular Mechanics*

I hope you can avoid the trap of making a big investment you soon dislike, but if you find yourself living with someone else's big investment, I hope you can find playful ways to make it work for you. Your home should express you, and you're a living being who changes in response to your thoughts and experiences. So your home should leave you room to evolve and change.

But, more importantly, it should inspire you to think of yourself and your life in new ways and challenge you to grow.

MAKING A SCENE IN THE FOYER

Now, for the fun stuff inside.

The front door to the house opens into a small foyer. The visitor walks through the door and faces a wall that stands between two Corinthian columns. The wall was covered in ivory textured paper.

I wanted to use the wall to create a little drama and make a statement: get ready for some fun. The large tiles in the marble floor have a classic gray-and-ivory pattern with black accents. I've always liked that floor, and I wanted to highlight its beauty.

First to go was the wallpaper, which was stained and peeling in some places. I found an inexpensive electric steamer called a Wagner Spraytech. Just add distilled water to it, and it works well with no chemicals. The steamer did its job, and buying it beat having to rent a steamer and return it after a few days.

I found an online paint store called Clare Paint that delivers its premium products straight to the customer's door, along with rollers, pans, and everything else people need to transform

Photo 10. The foyer, "before," looked something like this. A foyer's job is to welcome guests to the house and ignite their curiosity about what lies beyond.

a room.[53] Clare paints are formulated to be zero VOC,[54] ultralow odor, and eco-friendly; and they cover walls and trim beautifully. Clare also sends customers peel-and-stick samples of the colors, as Samplize does. I painted the wall in a warm taupe called On Point

53   Clare: Online Paint Store, House Paint & Supplies Delivered (clare.com)

54   Volatile organic compounds (VOCs) are emitted as gases from certain liquids or solids. VOCs include a variety of chemicals, some of which may have short- and long-term adverse health effects. Concentrations of many VOCs are consistently higher indoors (up to ten times higher) than outdoors. See https://www.epa.gov/.

Photo 11. Foyer in progress. Table with Bailey-style turned legs. Table made by carpenter Isaac Ott. I chose the dark mahogany stain for the table to highlight the black accents in the marble floor.

by Clare Paint. I chose a neutral color because I planned to hang a fabric backdrop on the wall, and I wanted the paint color to work with any fabric I chose. Also, On Point is warm without a yellow cast that would have made the room look dingy in low light.

I found table legs I liked online at the Carolina Leg Company.[55] They're turned legs in a dramatic style called Bailey, and the legs are pine.[56] The playful bulbousness of the design enchants me, with a fanciful quality that invites guests to wonder what other surprises await them. I hired a carpenter and asked him to build a table around the legs and stain

---

55 Handcrafted Wooden Table Legs | Modern Furniture Legs (carolinalegco.com)

56 James + James in Springdale, Arkansas, also makes custom fine furniture with Bailey-turned legs. See https://carpenterjames.com/

THE ROOMS INSIDE

Photo 12. Foyer, "after." We installed a curtain rod to hang the shibori fabric tablecloth as a backdrop. The rod's brackets are adjustable, so we were able to bring it close to the wall. I made a rod pocket at one end of the fabric and hung it from the rod. The result is a wall hanging that doesn't sag in the middle and lays almost flush against the wall.

Table legs: Bailey turned legs by Carolina Leg Company (carolinalegco.com)
Wall hanging: Tie-dye tablecloth, shibori indigo by sunny_afternoon, cotton sateen tablecloth (spoonflower.com)
Curtain rod: Kamanina one-inch curtain rod
Sculptures by scotdonadi0 (eBay)
Wall: On Point by Clare Paint (clare.com)

DESIGN FOR YOUR MIND · 43

Photo 13. Foyer, "after." The shibori fabric backdrop highlights the sculptures and the antique brass curios that came from my maternal grandmother.

Backdrop: Tie-dye tablecloth, Shibori Indigo by sunny_afternoon, cotton sateen tablecloth (spoonflower.com)
Sculptures by scotdonadi0 (eBay)

it in a dark mahogany color that echoes the black accents in the marble floor and draws attention to the floor. I love the results.

As a centerpiece, I found a large sculpture on eBay made by an artist in Goleta, California. I admire his work and have several of his pieces. They're sort of pre-Columbian and modern at the same time.

I spent months searching for a fabric backdrop that captivated me and hinted at other discoveries to be made in the house. I finally found what I wanted at a company called Spoonflower. The fabric wall hanging with the indigo shibori pattern you see in Photo 12 is a cotton sateen tablecloth made by an artist whose work is offered through Spoonflower. I made a rod pocket at one end and hung it from a curtain rod.

Photo 14. The den, "before." Removing the clutter and replacing the dark curtains were giant steps toward bringing this room alive.

THE DEN: CREATING THE PERFECT PLACE FOR PLAY AND WORK

GETTING STARTED

The den was a stumper. The curtains dated from well before the late 1990s, when my parents had moved into the house. The sofa and armchairs had traveled with my parents from house to house in their moves over the years. The rest of the room was stuffed with knickknacks, framed pictures, and books. After the appraiser submitted his report, my siblings and I worked out a system for choosing the things each of us wanted to keep. Then, everything else that the auctioneer thought would sell went to auction, and what remained was donated, given away, or tossed, if necessary.

My goal was to reimagine the den as a room that holds memories without being cluttered. I gave the curtains to a mechanic friend who now lies on them as he works under cars. Neither the siblings nor the auctioneer wanted the sofa and armchairs, though they were in good condition, notwithstanding their age. I donated them to a local nonprofit that gives vouchers to families and makes a warehouse full of donated furniture available for them to choose from. Much of what we donated from the den and the rest of the house—unselected books, knickknacks, clothing, and dishes—went to Vietnam Veterans of America (VVA).[57] VVA lets private companies bid on the items each year, and the funds raised support VVA's local, state, and national programs benefitting Vietnam and other veterans. I scheduled pickups on VVA's website, and on the day, I left the boxes at my front door. There was no charge. It was that easy.

I wanted to create a relaxing place where I could stretch out to read, write, think, and spend time with friends. I aimed to keep it free of clutter but fill it with life. So I designed it with furniture and other objects that give me comfort and inspire me to think and feel.

CHOOSING THE PAINT COLORS

For the walls, I chose a warm gray by Clare Paint called Windy City. The trim features intricate molding, and I chose Whipped, also by Clare Paint. Because the natural light in the den is not as bright as the light outside the house, and because I wanted the trim to look fresh and not dingy, I didn't risk as much yellow as was safe to use on the exterior trim of the house. But, because the house is a hundred years old and the details are faithful to their period, I also wanted to avoid the modern and slightly cold look of stark, white trim.

---

57 "Pickup Please : Help Our Vets - We Pickup Your Donations

A FEW TIPS TO MANAGE SAD

Designing a room to take advantage of natural light, and using paint colors and finishes that reflect natural light, can support the well-being of people living with seasonal affective disorder (SAD). SAD is a recurrent depressive disorder with a seasonal pattern, usually beginning in fall and continuing into winter months. The causes of SAD are complex, but research suggests a link to the overproduction of the sleep hormone melatonin. The body normally produces melatonin throughout the day and makes more when it's dark to trigger drowsiness as a signal to sleep. In the winter, less sunlight and shorter days trigger the body to produce more melatonin. But people with seasonal affective disorder are thought to overproduce melanin when days are shorter and darker, leading to symptoms of depression, including sadness, lack of energy, loss of interest in usual activities, and carbohydrate cravings. Seasonal Affective Disorder: What You Should Know | Johns Hopkins Medicine

Whipped by Clare has just a touch of warmth. It's perfect for the molding and for the other trim in the den.

The west-facing and the big south-facing windows in the den offer plenty of natural light. I chose a sectional sofa for chatting and stretching out to read and write next to the window that faces west. When the afternoon sun shines bright through the west-facing window, I can close the curtains and still enjoy the indirect natural light that comes through the south-facing window.

When I'm reading or writing in natural light, as opposed to artificial light, I can lose myself for hours. That's a good thing. Creativity and intellectual activity require persistence, and persistence requires the time needed for extended focus. If you want to read and create and think in a space, it helps to set it up so that you're comfortable and refreshed by it. You want to spend the time in there that enables you to persist through multiple drafts and the extended thinking necessary to create.[58]

THE WORLD OUTSIDE

But what we see and hear through that window also matters. The birds and squirrels that enchant us as we read or work help keep us going.[59] Attention restoration theory holds that exposure to nature relieves mental fatigue. The songs of birds are a powerful connection to nature, and their songs surround us even if we live in urban environments.[60] The sight of birds at a feeder outside my window soothes my soul.

And then there are the trees. Those patterns replicated in a tree on different scales—the trunk and branches of the tree, the individual branches supporting smaller branches, and the veins of the leaves themselves—are called fractals. Fractals are patterns that repeat at different scales, and nature is full of them. Research shows that the human preference for fractals is driven by a balance between increased arousal (a desire for engagement and complexity) and decreased tension (a desire for relaxation or refreshment).[61] In other words, people find the sight of a tree stimulating and comforting at the same time. As for human-made fractals, I have always thought Russian nesting dolls were cool. Now I know why.

---

58 "Creativity, Inspiration, and Persistence," Darin Hayton, https://dhayton.haverford.edu/blog/2012/03/14/creativity-Inspiration-and-persistence

59 "A Focus on Nature: The Attention Restoration Theory," Human Spaces

60 "How to Enjoy the Benefits of Nature Without Ever Leaving Your Home," SELF

61 "Aesthetics and Psychological Effects of Fractal Based Design," *Frontiers*

CREATING MOVEMENT AND TEXTURE

I wanted to make the room cozy, but I didn't want to feel (or to have my guests feel) trapped, physically or mentally. One way to keep people from feeling that way is to encourage their eyes to move. Rather than design a room that presents itself as a still life, why not present it as a moving picture and let the person who enters participate in the movement?

An easy way to do this is to choose a target for the eye, a focal point. Then, as the eye travels to the focal point and away from it, it sweeps up other interesting objects, along with their shapes, colors, and textures.

As you'll see in Photo 15, the focal point I chose is the vivid blue, orange, and red canvas painting in the far right-hand corner of the room, hung at a diagonal line from the entrance. The piece is a reproduction of a color-field work by Mark Rothko, the twentieth-century American abstract expressionist I mentioned earlier. Rothko uses floating planes of vibrant color to tap into our most basic emotions and speak to the fundamental nature of what he called the "human drama." [62] I love the flash of the molten orange rod that seems to ignite the red that borders the canvas and the gradual brightening of the blue as it travels from the lower left to the upper right-hand corner. This work fires my imagination as it grounds me. It gives me hope.

Directly beneath the canvas in the line of vision is a large ikat[63] throw pillow. Then the eye might travel to the left of the canvas and take in the bookshelf with its vibrant glass vases and sculptures and the silk ficus tree, or it might travel to the right and take in the other throw pillows on the sofa, the window and the view outside, the round glass coffee table, and the geometric-patterned rug.

---

62 "Mark Rothko: Introduction," *National Gallery of Art*

63 Ikat (pronounced ee-kaht) is an Indonesian resist-dyeing technique. Fabric manufacturers today incorporate ikat-style patterns into textiles even if they don't use the resist-dyeing technique. The ikat-style pattern is characterized by a slightly blurry repetition of simple shapes.

But the eye has taken a journey that it was invited to by the vivid colors in the painting. The eye, and the mind behind the eye, are encouraged to move and explore, not settle in one place.

Because I wanted the eye to be drawn to the painting and bookshelf, I wanted to keep it from stopping before it arrived at its destination. So I chose the coffee table for its soft lines and transparency and placed it in the crook of the sectional sofa. The eye passes right through the coffee table on its path to the painting and the bookshelf. I chose the large blue-and-white embroidered throw pillow with the ikat-style pattern for its large scale, texture, and bold design.[64] The large solid-blue throw pillow is velvet. Texture is important. Touching velvet and other soft materials, such as a fleece blanket, is thought to reduce stress by stimulating the release of oxytocin,[65] a calming hormone. We have oxytocin receptors in our hands.[66]

Another way to keep from feeling trapped is to make sure we're not stuck in a time warp. So I blended antiques with modern details. The artwork combines modern minimalism with framed nineteenth-century prints of sofas that French furniture makers offered customers as a sort of catalog. And, to avoid feeling physically stuck, I added a wicker chair that swivels and two ottomans that can be moved around. I store a fleece blanket inside one of them and pull it over me when I stretch out to read.

64 "What Is Ikat? All About the Traditional Indonesian Dyeing Technique," *House Beautiful*
65 "Oxytocin: The love hormone," *Harvard Health*
66 "The Science of Holding Hands," *British Columbia Medical Journal*

THE ROOMS INSIDE

Photo 15. Den, "after." The vivid colors in the canvas that hangs in the far corner draw the eye in a diagonal line from the door and invite it to travel to objects to the left and right of the canvas. The crook of the sectional sofa creates a corner that makes the den feel cozy.

ADDING DRAMA TO THE BOOKSHELVES

After the walls and trim were painted, I organized my books by subject and placed them on the shelves, along with sculptures and glass vases. But, as you see below, the contents of the shelves looked dull against the white background.

Because the bookshelves are in the direct line of vision as we enter the room, and because the items themselves deserve to be highlighted, I repainted the backs of the shelves with At Sea by Benjamin Moore in semigloss. At Sea is an aqua color, and it plays well with the blues, reds, and greens in the room. It also makes the objects on the shelves pop.

DESIGN FOR YOUR MIND · 51

THE ROOMS INSIDE

Photo 16. Den bookshelf, "before." The objects on the shelves disappear into the white background.

Photo 17. Den and bookcase, "after." Now the objects on the shelves look more vivid. And, because the two bookcases are in the direct line of vision from the entrance to the room, the aqua shade gives the entire room a lift. I found the large rust colored ceramic pitcher you see in the left-hand bookcase on Etsy. It came from a shop in Ukraine.

Walls: Windy City by Clare Paint (clare.com)
Trim and body of bookcase: Whipped by Clare Paint (clare.com)
Inside bookcase: At Sea by Benjamin Moore
Sheet music collage screen from a thrift shop
Inside shelves: At Sea by Benjamin Moore in semigloss
(Left to right): Glass decanter from an antiques store; ceramic vase from Sydney, Australia; aqua glass vase from IKEA; retired modernist Salong handblown twelve-inch turquoise blue glass vase from allthingsfunandvintage (eBay.com); ceramic pitcher from VintageItemsShopUA (etsy.com); sculpture by scotdonadi0 (eBay.com); Saybrook swivel chair (grandinroad.com) Emery linen matte black grommet blackout curtains (potterybarn.com)

Photo 18. The den, "after." Thanks to the abundant natural light, soothing colors and textures, the greenery, and the comfortable sofa, the den is my favorite place to read and write.

Emery linen matte black grommet blackout curtains (potterybarn.com)
On right bookshelf: Vintage handblown art glass Blenko-style teal round vase;
eight-by-eight-inch vase from kathysplace (eBay.com);
sculpture by scotdonadi0 (eBay.com);
small aqua vase from a thrift store
Canvas art: Mark Rothko Reproduction, Blue, Orange, Red Canvas by StoneofArts (etsy.com);
Sofa: Rencher sofa and chaise by Mercury Row (Wayfair.com)
Throw pillows (from left): Delancey embroidered throw pillow (Pottery Barn), Thibaut Austin striped pillow in blue by PillowFever (etsy.com), and indigo blue velvet pillow by LovePillowArt (etsy.com);
Table: Saskya four-legs coffee table with storage (wayfair.com).
Rug: Nazca Calva rectangular cream, light tan (rugsdirect.com).
Walls: Windy City (clare.com). Trim and body of bookshelves: Whipped (clare.com).
Inside bookcase: At Sea by Benjamin Moore

A RELAXING SPACE FOR WORK, TOO

Within a week of making these renovations, I discovered I could work happily in the den for hours. So I rethought my plans for another room in the house we call the study. I had planned to work in the study, but it turns out the den has everything I need to stay focused: natural light, access to Wi-Fi, and most importantly, a comfortable and roomy sectional sofa. I can put my feet up, laptop on my lap, and lose myself in a project. The antique slant-top desk stores office items—such as staplers—out of sight, the closet with shelves stores binders, and I can straighten up the room in minutes. I imagined the den as a place to relax and play, but it also turns out to be the perfect workspace, where I work better because I am relaxed.

We'll talk about the study room later and the important purpose it still serves. But I do my real work in the den.

MAKING ROOM FOR MEMORIES

In the photo below, you see a small table with turned legs. I inherited that table from my maternal grandmother. I have liked that table since I was a child, and I love having reminders of my grandmother in my renovated house. The lamp on top of the table is a vase that my grandmother's parents brought home from China and turned into a table lamp. It is another of my lifelong favorites. Items that come from past generations remind me of family members I have loved and help keep them with me. And they acquaint me with family members I never knew. Combining the old with the new grounds me in the present and helps clear my mind as I look ahead.

Photo 19. The den, '"after." The side table with turned legs and the table lamp came from my maternal grandmother. The antique slant-top desk to the right stores a stapler and hole punch, notebooks, my laptop, and any documents I'm working on. It's easy to stash these items in the desk when I'm not working and keep the room neat. My printer and file cabinets stay in the study. Thanks to Wi-Fi, I can print my documents from the den. And I'm more focused and creative when I'm not surrounded by a lot of office equipment.

FILLING A ROOM WITH ART, BOOKS, FAMILY HEIRLOOMS, AND NATURE HELPS ME FEEL CONNECTED TO LIFE—EVEN AS I ENJOY MY SOLITUDE.

THE ROOMS INSIDE

Photo 20. The den, "after."

Clockwise from left: Delancey embroidered throw pillow (Pottery Barn), Thibaut Austin striped pillow in blue by PillowFever (etsy.com), and indigo blue velvet pillow by LovePillowArt (etsy.com)

SUPPORTING SMALL BUSINESSES

I love to support small businesses. Purchasing custom-made throw pillows on Etsy is a good way to do this. I read reviews before I order, and every time I place an order on Etsy, the vendor provides me with meticulous workmanship and attentive customer service.

Photo 21. Den mantel area, "before." To eliminate the clutter on the mantel, I turned the hall area near the kitchen into a photo gallery. Guests can browse the photos while I'm cooking.

ONE STATEMENT PIECE ON THIS MANTEL. THAT'S IT.

I would rather display family photos in a single area that I can designate as a gallery. This frees up space in the den and other rooms where framed photos tend to congregate, and it reduces clutter and dusting. As you'll see in Photo 23, I replaced the photos with original artwork and a large, antique gilt mirror I'd brought from my previous house. The frame is imposing, and it creates enough of a spectacle on its own that I saw no need to add other object to the mantel. I kept it simple.

THE ROOMS INSIDE

Photo 22. The canvas painting to the left of the mantel was created by my friend Deborah Finco. The painting faces me as I do my work, and I can lose myself in it. The deep water transfixes me, and the large cloud looming above seems to swirl and move and promise some change in the weather.

Into the Deep Blue, acrylic on stretched canvas by Deborah Finco (Deborah Finco Art on Facebook)

THE ROOMS INSIDE

Photo 23. The den, "after." The mirror on the mantel is imposing enough not to need any other embellishments. And there's plenty to look at on the bookshelves along the far wall.

Clockwise from left: Into the Deep Blue, acrylic on stretched canvas by Deborah Finco (Deborah Finco Art on Facebook);
sheet music collage screen from a thrift shop; Saybrook swivel chair (grandinroad.com);
aqua glass vase on bookshelf from IKEA, retired modernist Salong handblown;
twelve-inch turquoise blue glass vase from allthingsfunandvintage (eBay.com);
sculpture on bookshelf by scotdonadi0 (eBay.com);
ceramic pitcher on bookshelf by VintageItemsShopUA (etsy.com)
Walls: Windy City by Clare Paint (clare.com)
Trim and bookshelf: Whipped by Clare Paint (clare.com)
Inside bookshelf: At Sea by Benjamin Moore
Rug: Nazca Calva rectangular cream, light tan (rugsdirect.com)

Photo 24. Den, "after." Before we mounted the screen on the wall, we fortified the back to make it one solid piece. That way, the two hinged sides won't buckle into each other. Then we mounted the screen on the wall beside the fireplace.

SHEET MUSIC AS WALL ART

I found the screen in the photo above in a thrift shop. It's a collage some clever person made with antique sheet music. On the left-hand panel, the screen's creator placed sheet music for pianoforte by nineteenth-century German composer Carl Maria von Weber. The sheet music was inscribed with a handwritten note that reads: "To my dear cousin Janet with love from Katie Edith Smith. August 5, 1896." How cool is that?

Photo 25. The den, "after." I chose a rug with a geometric pattern that's powerful in its simplicity.

BRINGING IT ALL TOGETHER

The den is now my favorite place to spend time with friends, stream movies, watch football (my new passion!), and work on this book. I feel at peace in this room—energized but not rattled, focused, and not distracted by clutter or the to-do list in my head. I love hearing friends describe the peace and energy they feel in this room. And I'm reading books I always wanted to read.

Photo 26. Atrium, "before." Like the foyer, the atrium sets the tone for the house. It's the first large room guests see when they come into the house, and they must pass through the atrium to enter other rooms.

THE ATRIUM

On the other side of the foyer wall is the atrium. It's the first large room guests see when they enter the house, and they must pass through it to enter the den and the living room. The photo above shows the atrium as it looked before. The walls are crowded with framed photos and mementos. The mantel is cluttered. The white latticework on the walls doesn't work with the more contemporary furnishings. The walls themselves are a dull gray. The flowered sofa and armchairs are too sweet for the cool and unsentimental porcelain tile floor.

I wanted to combine modern with classic to welcome guests to the house and create a setting where I could sit and relax with them.

Photo 27. The atrium, "after." The blue-gray color on the walls invites us to breathe as it coaxes the eye to travel upward.

Clockwise from left: White loveseat: Ameriya Southview upholstered loveseat; glass-top coffee table from Crate and Barrel; aqua glass vase, vintage IKEA handblown turquoise vase, retired 1980s, from fri_4605; accent chair, chunky woven petite accent chair (anthropologie.com); dark-gray loveseat, Ameriya fifty-inch upholstered loveseat; throw pillow, white with black dashed cross African mudcloth pillow by MackenzieBryantCo (etsy.com); print fabric chair, Noemi charcoal gray and ivory dash print chair (worldmarket.com;).
Rug: NuLOOM jute rug in silver
Walls: First Snowfall by Benjamin Moore
Mark Rothko canvas art reproduction by LorienProCanvas (etsy.com)
Velener artificial plant, outdoor agave

THE ROOMS INSIDE

Photo 28. The atrium, "after." For the accent wall behind the white loveseat, I chose Silver Mist by Benjamin Moore. Silver Mist is a slightly darker tone of First Snowfall, the color we used on the walls. The result calls attention to the accent wall without allowing it to dominate the room.

Clockwise from left: Concrete end table, pedestal end table by 17 Stories;
white loveseat, Ameriya Southview upholstered loveseat;
throw pillow, dash line African mudcloth pillow by MackenzieBryantCo (etsy.com);
accent chair, chunky woven petite accent chair (anthropologie.com);
dark-gray loveseat, Ameriya fifty-inch upholstered loveseat;
throw pillow, white with black dashed cross African mudcloth pillow by MackenzieBryantCo (etsy.com);
print fabric chair, Noemi charcoal gray and ivory dash print chair (worldmarket.com)
Rug: NuLOOM jute rug in silver
Walls: First Snowfall by Benjamin Moore
Accent Wall: Silver Mist by Benjamin Moore

Photo 29. The mantel, "after." I kept the mantel area simple to keep the focus on the mirror that my father made.

Clockwise from left: Barometer from an antiques store; standing iron candelabra from a thrift shop; silk fern; homemade mirror; sculpture by scotdonadi0 (eBay.com); aqua glass vase, vintage Blenko handblown crackle vase glass art teal from upnorthtreasure (eBay.com); red vase from a thrift store; framed botanical art from an antiques store; silk topiary; Mark Rothko canvas art reproduction by LorienProCanvas (etsy.com); Velener artificial plant, outdoor agave

STARTING WITH THE WALLS

We took down the latticework and painted the walls from floor to ceiling with a blue-gray color by Benjamin Moore called First Snowfall. As you see in Photo 27, the ceiling is thirty feet high, and the color mimics the sky, inviting the eye to travel upward to the skylights. I feel free when I look at this color, as I do when I gaze at the sky and realize its infinite space.

STYLIN' THE MANTEL

I remember the day my dad made the wood-framed mirror you see over the fireplace in the photo below. I was eight or nine, and Dad hung the mirror over the sideboard in the dining room of the house our family lived in when I was growing up. I have always liked that mirror, and I wanted it to be one of the first things guests see when they walk into this room.

I decided to use the mirror my dad built as an anchor for the mantel area, and I didn't want an arrangement to overwhelm it. The mantel area doesn't need to command attention, anyway; the room has other focal points and plenty to look at, so a minimalist arrangement that packed some drama was all it needed.

The mantel area encompasses more than the mantel shelf. It takes in the area on either side of the fireplace and extends a few feet beyond. The area also stretches below the mantel shelf to the fireplace and the area on either side of it.

In Photo 29, you see two points of greenery—the fern and the topiary—each in a different shape. I placed five objects on the mantel, if you count the standing candelabra with candles reaching above the surface of the mantel shelf. The odd number creates an asymmetry that is inherently dramatic. Even numbers create symmetry, and as I mentioned earlier, the orderliness of symmetry comforts the brain. But odd numbers are powerful, and keeping things a little off-balance creates drama. In fact, I didn't position anything in the center of the mantel, instead arranging objects to either side and making sure each was a distinct size, shape, color, and texture. Layering objects is another way to add depth and interest.

But, to stay low-key, I kept the layering to a minimum, only positioning the fern so it covered a small corner of the mirror. Even the candles in the candelabra are white. The only pops of color are the small aqua glass vase on the right side of the mantel shelf and the tall, narrow red vase beside it.

Photo 30. Atrium, "after." The jute rug is interwoven with metallic silver threads that make the rug dressier and more interesting than a plain jute rug.

Clockwise from left: Noemi charcoal gray and ivory dash print chair (worldmarket.com); white loveseat, Ameriya Southview upholstered loveseat; throw pillows, dash line African mudcloth pillow; white and black dashed cross African mudcloth pillow by MackenzieBryantCo (etsy.com); dark-gray loveseat, Ameriya fifty-inch upholstered loveseat; aqua glass vase, Vintage IKEA handblown turquoise vase, retired 1980s, from fri_4605 (ebay.com); green glass vase from a thrift shop; ceramic dish circa 1992 by Sylvia Wyler (boathousepottery.com) Rug: NuLOOM jute rug in silver

THE SEATING AREA

To create a place to relax and have snacks and drinks with guests, I went with mid-century modern upholstered furniture that pairs well with the antiques and formal artwork. Because the atrium is the first large room guests see, and it provides access to other rooms in the house, I chose sofas and a chair that would not look "sat-in" after use. I read customer reviews carefully to make sure the furniture I chose offered firm seating. The two-tiered glass coffee

Photo 31. Ceramic dish circa 1992 by Sylvia Wyler (boathousepottery.com).

table is no-fuss, and it's a good place to display two of my favorite pieces of vintage glass art and a ceramic dish made by a professional potter who is the sister of an old friend.

SCALE: GOING BIG IN A BIG ROOM

The far wall of the atrium called for outsize plants, urns, and artwork because the high ceiling and large room would swallow conventionally sized objects. This was the place for the hundred-pound concrete urn that had sat in my garage for twenty years, the five-headed water lily plant I'd purchased for the tiny galley kitchen in the guesthouse, a big topiary, and a mammoth horizontal ikat painting. It can be fun to play with scale and go big with big objects in a small room, but, as you see in Photo 32, the far wall in a spacious room with high ceilings is the place for objects that won't disappear.

Photo 32. Atrium, "after." The soaring ceiling calls for oversize artwork against the far wall.

THE ROOMS INSIDE

Photo 33. Atrium, "after." I left most of the porcelain tile floor rug-free. Given the constant foot traffic through the atrium, life is easier with flooring that's easy to keep clean.

I LIKE TO TAKE ADVANTAGE OF A VERY HIGH CEILING WITH A BLUE THAT MIMICS THE SKY. THE COLOR DRAWS MY EYE UPWARD AND INVITES ME TO BREATHE.

Photo 34. Guest bathroom

REIMAGINING THE GUEST BATHROOM

Just off the foyer is a guest bathroom with a shower that features gold-veined black marble and ornate brass fixtures.

Photo 35. Guest bathroom. The gold-colored fixtures add classic detail.

I suspect my mom wanted to make the bathroom more cheerful by softening the look of the black marble. She had the original tile floor ripped out and replaced with beige linoleum. She also covered the walls with pink-and-blue flowered wallpaper.

I decided to take a different tack. I would embrace the black marble and modify the other details in the bathroom to complement it. We removed the linoleum and replaced the flooring with tiles in a classic black-and-white pattern that is typical of old houses in Europe.

We steamed off the wallpaper and painted the walls in On Point, the warm taupe I'd used on the accent wall in the foyer. We sanded the white cabinets and painted them in a darker shade of taupe by Clare Paint called Flatiron in semigloss.

I replaced the knobs on the cabinets with antique bronze pull rings to complement the classic tone of the floor and the black marble shower. I asked the carpenter to build a wooden frame to cover the metal frame of the contractor-grade mirror above the sink and paint the wooden frame black.

THE ROOMS INSIDE

Photo 36. Guest bathroom, "after." I didn't fight with the formal nature of the black marble shower and ornate gold fixtures. Instead, I welcomed them and figured out how to complement them with more compatible flooring and other details.

Photo 37. Guest bathroom, "after." I embraced the European tone of the black marble and gold fixtures with a classic black-and-white tile floor, a painting by a nineteenth-century Italian artist, an antique étagère that belonged to my grandmother, and gold and black antique etchings. I found lace panels at an antiques store and hung them over the window as a valance.

Framed pictures from an antiques store
Towel ring from Mobitell (etsy.com)
Canvas artwork: La Rotonda di Palmieri by Giovanni Fattori (greatbigcanvas.com)
Walls: On Point by Clare Paint (Clare.com)
Cupboards: Flatiron in semigloss by Clare Paint (Clare.com)
Tile floor: Betera Jet thirteen-by-thirteen-inch ceramic patterned wall and floor tile by EliteTile
Cupboard pull rings: ForgeHardwareStudio (etsy.com)

Above the mirror, I hung a canvas replica of a painting by nineteenth-century Italian artist Giovanni Fattori called *La Rotonda di Palmieri*. It depicts a group of demurely clad women in the shade of a canopy on a beach. I found a distinctive antique bronze towel ring and a towel bar at a shop on Etsy. The white hand towel with the black trim and tassels came from Target—on clearance. The mahogany étagère next to the sink came from my grandmother.

Celebrating the black marble, rather than removing it or denying its serious nature, saved me money and time. We painted the walls and cupboards, laid the tile, and transformed the room within a couple of weeks. Now the guest bathroom is one of my favorite rooms in the house, and when guests ask to use it, I'm glad to show them the way.

TAKING THE STUFFY OUT OF THE LIVING ROOM

TAKING STOCK

My brother used to call the living room the ballroom. The fixtures and the size and scale of the room announce that it expects to be taken seriously. The ceiling is fifteen feet high with massive Greek Ionic columns and intricate crown molding. The two large chandeliers date from the 1920s. A large portrait of one of our ancestors hangs over a nineteenth-century mahogany display cabinet. The Regency-style coffee table was so fragile that no one dared touch it.

This was the room that my siblings and I tiptoed through with our dinner plates on our way to the enclosed patio on the other side. No one came into the living room to sit and read or talk, unless it was Christmastime or Thanksgiving or some other family occasion when we'd sit on the sofa and listen to Mom play the piano and would sing along with her.

I wanted to treat the room with respect, but I wanted to refresh it in ways that left its stuffy days behind.

THE ROOMS INSIDE

Photo 38. Living room, "before." The size of the room and its Ionic columns, lofty ceiling, and large chandeliers convey its formal tone.

A NEW LOOK

The window treatments were the place to start. The curtains had been there when my parents moved into the house in the late 1990s, and the fabric was showing holes. I knew custom-made curtains would take weeks to arrive, so I gave the new curtains a head start while I worked on other areas of the living room. The old curtains went to my mechanic friend, so he can lie on them as he works under vehicles. Members of my neighborhood Facebook group recommended a small business that makes custom curtains, and the owner supplied what I wanted for the four large windows. The fabric I chose was an off-white linen blend, and I asked for a single-pinch pleat—formal, but not too serious.

Years ago, when my parents enclosed the open-air patio on the other side of the living room, they'd created a relaxing space for the family to celebrate birthdays and have dinners together, but the new walls had blocked much of the natural light that once flowed into the living room. The burgundy rugs, the dark blue sofa, and the dark wingback chairs made the room even darker.

I had three goals for the room: to bring in more light, to make the room feel more relaxed and friendly, and to accept and appreciate the room's formal nature.

I donated the dark blue sofa, the pink-flowered loveseats, and the four wingback chairs to the same nonprofit that had accepted the upholstered furniture in the den. The burgundy rugs went to the auctioneer. A nineteenth-century painting of a ship that had hung over the fireplace mantel went to my brother. In place of the painting, I hung a large, gilt-framed mirror to reflect light from the patio. I replaced the burgundy rugs with three identical blue-and-orange wool rugs with tasseled edges from Safavieh. The blue in the rugs is calming, and the orange accents add energy.[67] The tassels are just fun.

---

67   Orange pops against a blue background because orange and blue are complementary colors. That is, they sit opposite each other on the color wheel. "How to Use a Color Wheel Chart to Find Complementary Colors," *House Beautiful*

THE ROOMS INSIDE

Photo 39. Living room, "after." I found the salmon-colored barrel-back armchair (middle) in the basement. I believe it had been left behind by a former owner of the house whose attention to detail I recognize from other meticulous work she commissioned in the 1960s and 1970s. The workmanship shown in the upholstery is exquisite, and it would challenge my budget today.

Evelynn coffee table (jossandmain.com)
Aldridge forty-seven-inch cotton armless settee
Safavieh Aspen Collection handmade boho braided tassel wool rug

THE SEATING AREAS

The living room accommodates two seating areas. I chose glass-top coffee tables for both of them to make entertaining stress-free. There's no risk of water marks on glass, and unlike solid wood, it doesn't darken the room. The enclosed patio will always block some of the light from coming through the French doors, so I gravitated toward glass and mirrors, light-colored fabrics, and vivid colors.

First Seating Area

The Evelynn coffee table from Joss and Main that you see in Photo 39 is a dead ringer for a far more expensive one offered by a well-known, high-end furniture retailer. Thanks to customers' comments online pointing this out, I checked the high-end website and discovered that the Evelynn was *several thousand dollars less*. So I ordered it. What a coup. It's well-made and solid, with no assembly required. And heavy. Thank goodness, shipping was free.

The Evelynn doesn't compromise on quality, making it a perfect addition to my living room while keeping a significant amount of money in my pocket. As a bonus, my sister fell for the Evelynn when she saw mine, and she ordered one for her own house.

Second Seating Area

The Regency-style coffee table in the second seating area went to auction. I replaced it with a large, wrought-bronze, glass-top coffee table I'd bought from a private seller in upstate New York. I found the seller on aptdeco.com.[68]

---

68 Buy and Sell Used Furniture—We Pickup & Deliver - AptDeco

Photo 40. Living room, "after." The wrought-bronze coffee table was an heirloom belonging to a private seller in upstate New York. It's right at home here.

*Clockwise from left: Wrought-bronze glass-top coffee table (aptdeco.com);
Aldridge forty-seven-inch cotton armless settee;
off-white sofa, "reimagined" with dark stained frame and turned legs
Throw pillows (far left and far right): Anthonyson chevron cotton throw pillow; Reilly embroidered lumbar throw pillow (potterybarn.com);
round velvet pillow in strawberry from JoeBlake (etsy.com)
Safavieh Aspen Collection handmade boho braided tassel wool rug*

I recommend AptDeco at every opportunity. It lists high-quality used furniture owned by private sellers and enables buyers to purchase directly from the seller and arrange for shipping through the AptDeco website.

As you see in Photo 40, the coffee table looks as if it was made for this living room. It dates from early to mid-twentieth century, the same period as the chandeliers—and the third-party delivery service by Biffi Transport LLC was as white-glove and personable as

Photo 41. Living room, "after.' The reimagined living room still respects its formal features, but it's not inhibited by them. I now find the room light, happy, and free.

Clockwise from left: Aldridge forty-seven-inch cotton armless settee; Evelynn coffee table (jossandmain.com); salmon-colored barrel-back chair from the basement; Aldridge forty-seven-inch cotton armless settee; off-white sofa, "reimagined" with dark stained frame and turned legs Throw pillows (far left and far right): Anthonyson chevron cotton throw pillow; Reilly embroidered lumbar throw pillow (potterybarn.com); round velvet pillow in strawberry from JoeBlake (etsy.com) Wrought-bronze glass-top coffee table (aptdeco.com)

anything I have experienced. I paid less for the whole transaction, including delivery, than I would have paid for a replica of the coffee table if I had purchased it new.

The AptDeco website gives customers the option to search by category—say, sofa or mirror—and also by retailer. If you're looking for used furniture from Anthropologie or RH,[69] you can find it there.

Remember what we did in the den to encourage the eye to travel? I did the same thing in the living room, but this time, with the salmon-colored, upholstered, barrel-back armchair

---

69 Formerly, Restoration Hardware

Photo 42. Living room, "after." I tend to avoid matching throw pillows. But the textured ivory pillows at both ends frame the two pillows between them and add a touch of informality.

Far left and far right: Anthonyson chevron cotton throw pillow; Reilly embroidered lumbar throw pillow (potterybarn.com); round velvet pillow in strawberry from JoeBlake (etsy.com)

from the basement. And again, the entrance near a corner of the room provides the perfect setup. I take advantage of the long diagonal line to the opposite far corner and place a focal point, the armchair, in a color that will draw the eye. Then, as the eye travels to the armchair, it sweeps up the off-white sofa, the coffee table, rugs, throw pillows, loveseats, and maybe the painting and china cabinet in the background—anything that is in the eye's path to the armchair. Above the armchair is a round antique convex mirror that came from my grandmother. The placement of the mirror draws the eye upward.

The round velvet throw pillow on the off-white sofa was a find. I went hunting on Etsy for a round velvet pillow in a vibrant strawberry, and I found this one. Not only is it the right color to catch the eye as it travels to the armchair, but it's the only round pillow in the room, and its shape echoes the shape of the convex mirror on the wall behind the armchair. As a result, the pillow, the mirror, and the armchair help frame the other objects.

I find that when I stand in the doorways of the living room and the den, I breathe more easily and feel a little freer. It might be because I feel as if I'm moving, and that movement gives me energy.

THE SOFA: FIXING MY MISTAKE

About that off-white, mid-century modern sofa you see in the photo below. I fell in love with the sofa's flared arms on the manufacturer's website and decided to take the leap and order it. The sofa was a bit pricey, but I thought it would be worth the investment and the three-month wait for delivery.

Photo 43. Mid-century modern sofa, "before." This was how the sofa looked when it arrived. The flared arms are somewhat unusual, and I knew they'd add panache to the living room.

NEXT PAGE: Photo 44. Mid-century modern sofa, "after." We gave the frame a dark stain to match the dark turned legs. The contrast between the dark stain and the ivory upholstery makes the sofa interesting. I'm not concerned that the turned legs disrupt the sofa's mid-century modern vibe. I bought the sofa for its graceful, flared arms that work well in the formal living room.

But, as soon as the sofa arrived, I saw my mistake. The off-white upholstery paired with the pine-colored frame offered no contrast that would have added character. And as you see in Photo 43, the pine-colored legs were plain—a good fit with its mid-century modern vibe but out of place in my living room with its dark-colored, ornately designed antiques. The sofa was made to order and couldn't be returned. And the purchase was my mistake—not the company's. I had to figure out how to fix it.

I thought about staining the pine-colored frame a dark walnut color and replacing the legs with something dark and interesting. But I couldn't think of a way to keep the off-white upholstery fabric from drinking up the dark stain as I applied it. Then Kurt and I turned the sofa on its side and discovered—yay!—that the wooden frame had been bolted onto the upholstered structure. That was great news. It meant the frame could be unbolted and removed for sanding and staining. So that's what we did.

I found turned sofa legs online. It turns out that people often need to replace the legs of sofas and chairs so they can raise or lower their furniture's height to accommodate their own, make it easier to get in and out, or create a fresh look. Sofa and chair legs are available in different heights, colors, and styles designed to be screwed into the frame.

I ordered eight-inch, turned, hardwood legs in dark walnut, and we stained the frame to match the legs.[70] I love the sofa now. And I was tickled when my sister, who didn't know the story, walked into the living room. Her first words were, "Wow. What a beautiful sofa." Score.

---

70   BingLTD eight-inch coffee profile hardwood sofa leg, set of eight

Photo 45. The lion chair, "before." This type of chair is more properly known as a dragon lion armchair, a Chinese carved dragon chair, or simply a dragon chair. The theme dates to ancient times when the dragon was a symbol of imperial power, and only the emperor was permitted to sit on a chair with a dragon carving.

THE LION CHAIR

Poor lion chair. The carved dragon lion armchair was another heirloom that my great-grandparents had brought back from China, where my great-grandfather had been stationed as a surgeon with the US Navy in the early 1900s.

I had liked the chair since I was a child, but when my siblings and I took turns choosing furniture from our late grandmother's house and our parents' estate, my sister chose the

Photo 46. Lion chair, "after." It gets plenty of love in the living room now. In fact, my niece likes to tease my sister for giving it up.

chair. The lion chair, as we called it fondly, hadn't been loved in a while. The wood frame was falling apart. The bottom had collapsed, and the springs and stuffing were dragging almost to the floor. Photo 45 captures the lion chair in its doleful state.

A few weeks after my sister chose it, she called and proposed a trade for something else she wanted. The lion chair was mine. I chose a fabric called Double Coverage Seaglass by Carole Fabrics[71] and the work was done by an upholsterer who brought decades of experi-

---

71   Double Coverage Seaglass by Carole Fabric - Fabric Carolina

ence from the old country. The fabric I chose has a performance count of fifteen thousand double rubs, making it well-suited for light to moderate use in the living room.

A performance count (aka rub count) measures the durability of a fabric, and in the United States, it's measured by a machine that simulates the effect of real-life rubbing on the material's surface, known as the Wyzenbeek method.[72] It's worth investigating the rub count of any fabric to make sure it will stand up to its intended use before spending good money on it. The article at the footnote below provides rub count ranges for different levels of use.[73]

MOM'S PIANO

Mom was born with an unusual musical ear. She revealed her gift at the age of four when she climbed onto her family's piano bench and offered a perfect rendition of the piece her ten-year-old brother had been practicing, with some frustration, for his lesson.

That's not entirely true. First, she played the piece with her brother's mistakes, over and over—sweetly subversive, even at four. Then she played the piece perfectly. To this day, I don't know if my grandparents recognized that their only daughter was a prodigy, or if, in the male-revering Naval Academy culture into which Mom was born in the early 1930s, her talents drew only casual attention. Certainly, Mom was never shopped around to Russian masters or other old-world émigrés who might have nurtured her gifts and provided the formal training that would have allowed them to flourish before a wider audience.

Perhaps that was just as well; Mom was left alone to develop her ear and her (to my mind) strangely mathematical understanding of chords and keys. Her gifts became the source of a lifelong private joy, and she was left free to share them with any audience she chose. And share them she did—with her family, her friends, and anyone who would appreciate them.

---

72 "Certified Wyzenbeek Abrasion Testing System and Testing Procedures," *NextGen Material Testing*
73 "Durability - Why Rub Count is Important," *The Sofa Review*

Mom had only to hear a complex work of classical music once before she rendered it in full form, by ear. In a flash, Mom could transpose a tune she was playing into another key to accommodate the vocal ranges of her children. We were fiercely proud of her. When my sister and I were little, we'd twirl around the living room in our sequined thrift-store tutus; we were ballerinas on a stage as Mom's hands rolled up and down the keyboard and she lost herself in Rachmaninoff's "Second Concerto" or Chopin's "Ocean Etude No. 12." I would open the front door wide, so the neighborhood kids could hear her.

Over the years, as our dad's career led the family to relocate to various cities, Mom founded volunteer singing groups in each new community. She would direct and accompany the groups on piano, and she and the group members would sing at nursing homes and prisons.

My brother liked to tell a story about Mom and a song by Led Zeppelin called "Kashmir." One night when he was a teenager, my brother was driving home to our parents' house as he blasted "Kashmir" on the car radio. He was still singing as he walked through the front door. Our mom was sitting at the piano, and he came in to give her a kiss. Mom asked what my brother was singing, and he offered his best rendition of "Kashmir," complete with crashing chords and key and tempo changes. Mom began fiddling as my brother went to his bedroom. When he came back into the living room, Mom was pounding out "Kashmir" in full form. It was classic Mom. Our family loves that story. We love that our mom, brilliant herself, appreciated the genius of Led Zeppelin, as illuminated by the vocal stylings of her teenage son. And that our brother, who was only three when "Kashmir" was released, could do justice to this complex song with nothing more than his voice and his passion.

Long after Mom had forgotten that Dad had died, that she didn't have a cat, that it was Christmas, or why she had begun a sentence, Mom remembered music. I made her a playlist on Spotify that featured her most lyrical favorites: "Moonlight Sonata," selections by Gershwin and Chopin, Barbra Streisand singing "Send in the Clowns," Pharrell Williams's "Happy," and Josh Groban delivering "You'll Never Walk Alone."

THE ROOMS INSIDE

Photo 47. Mom's piano is where it belongs.

When Mom lay in bed, too tired and confused to speak, I would ask her if she wanted to hear music. If she nodded yes, I would play her Spotify collection and watch her face as she listened. Mom would close her eyes, transported once again. Her eyelashes would flutter as she followed the melody and bathed in the warmth of the voices. Music was still her special friend.

But, one day, that friendship ended. Mom didn't want to listen to music anymore. She just wanted to sleep. Then she was gone.

Mom's baby grand piano stood in the corner of the living room, where I wanted it to stay in her honor. As my siblings and I moved through the selection process, I chose the piano, so the living room would always be its home.

DESIGN FOR YOUR MIND · 91

Photo 48. Kitchen, "before." The kitchen needed only a few cosmetic changes to give it personality. The accent tiles are lovely but a little tame for my taste.

REFRESHING THE KITCHEN

LOOKING FOR INSPIRATION

The kitchen needed some color and highlights and a facial—not a facelift. The layout was perfect for cooking and entertaining. Counter space abounded at the center island and on

Photo 49. Kitchen, "before." The white knobs disappear into the white cupboards. Larger knobs in a contrasting color would make them more interesting.

either side of the double sink, and the appliances were in fine shape. The Corian countertops[74] were in pristine condition, some twenty-five years after they had been installed.

But the walls, cupboards, center island, and countertops were all white. The only color was a ladylike blue painted inside the glass-front cupboards and in the blue-bordered accent tiles on the backsplash and above the countertops.

74   Corian is the brand name of a product introduced by DuPont in 1967. The generic term for Corian and other countertop products of the same composition is "solid surface." Solid Surface Countertops: Know Before You Buy," *The Spruce*

Photo 50. Kitchen, "before." Please excuse the mess. My sister and I were sorting and preparing items for donation. I took this photo to upload to the Benjamin Moore website as I was looking for the right paint color for the kitchen island. I include it here so you can see the "before" version of the island.

I wanted to broaden the color palette and give the room some edge and personality. I uploaded pictures of various areas of the kitchen on the Benjamin Moore website and experimented with colors for the walls, cupboards, and the island. I pored over kitchens on Pinterest, looking for photos that would spark a vision of my own.

My vision came to me slowly, over a couple of months. As it turned out, it was not difficult or expensive to execute.

GIVING MYSELF ELBOW ROOM

I wanted to give myself flexibility as I made changes, so I could shift course as my ideas developed without wasting money or effort. The accent tiles were an easy place to start. I didn't want

Photo 51. Kitchen, "before." The layout of the kitchen made cooking and entertaining easy and fun, so there was no need for the disruption and expense of a full kitchen remodel.

to risk removing them and damaging the surrounding tiles, so I found vinyl tile stickers on Etsy in a strong black-and-white geometric pattern that I could use as the foundation for the kitchen's new personality. I like the pattern so much that, at some point, I might decide to replace the stickers with porcelain tiles in the same pattern, but I don't know if that will ever be necessary.

The next easy and inexpensive change I made was to replace the flowered white knobs on the white cupboards and drawers with larger, solid-colored knobs in navy blue. The new knobs bring contrast and character.

To find the perfect color for the walls, I used the Benjamin Moore website to create mock-ups of the kitchen in more colors than I want to count, looking for the shade that excited me but

Photo 52. Kitchen, "after." The navy color of the island contrasts with the natural wood and metal elements in the room.

Clockwise from left: Counter chairs, Cesta rattan counter stool (cb2.com); seagrass wicker baskets with lids; vinyl accent tiles, SnazzyDecal (etsy.com) Pendant lamps: Savoy House Alden one-light in warm brass (amazon.com) Wall clock: milan_store (eBay) Walls: Wispy Green by Benjamin Moore Island: Goodnight Moon by Clare Paint (clare.com) Cupboard door pulls by JackAccessories (etsy.com)

that I wouldn't find overbearing in a few months. I finally fell in love with Wispy Green. It was just enough color to give the room a lift without being too chatty first thing in the morning.

Then I tackled the kitchen island. It was an obvious choice for a focal point, as a large fixture in the center of the room, but it needed to be painted in a strong color if it was to draw the eye. I decided that the solution was a dark navy blue with a little sheen. The winning color was Goodnight Moon by Clare Paint in semigloss. To add more drama, I dressed up the cupboard doors and drawers with distinctive pulls and knobs in antique brass.

Photo 52 shows a corner of the kitchen that is in a diagonal line from the entrance. The eye is drawn to the corner as one enters from outdoors, so it was a perfect place to create drama. I covered the white area above the refrigerator with the same black-and-white geometric tiles I'd used to cover the accent tiles on the wall.

The wall that faces the island was a natural accent wall that called for a paint color that struck a contrast with Wispy Green, a neutral-colored textured fabric covering, or some large and unexpected object. I experimented with options for weeks. I finally chose the latter and hung a massive, vintage-looking clockface. It was a simple solution, and it will

THE CORNER OF THE ROOM THAT LIES CATTY-CORNER TO THE ENTRANCE IS A PERFECT PLACE TO CREATE A SCENE. AS THE EYE IS PULLED ALONG THE DIAGONAL LINE TO THE CORNER, IT TAKES IN OTHER INTERESTING FEATURES OF THE ROOM ALONG THE WAY.

be easy to change if I ever decide to put up something else. That area of the kitchen island was also the right place to display the wooden cutting board that my brother had made me for Christmas.

NO CROWDS ON THIS ISLAND

One downside to a large center island is that it presents a big, centralized area where clutter can collect.

That was what happened to the island in its former life. It hosted a mishmash of trays and saucers that held orphaned keys, paper clips, rubber bands, old remotes, pieces of waxed fruit, mustard packets, an old fortune cookie, luggage tags, scraps of paper—the detritus of life.

Photo 53. Kitchen, "after." The vintage apothecary chest and the wicker baskets deliver a twofer: they're an easy way to keep things organized, and the natural wood and wicker give the room texture and warmth.

From left to right: Accent tiles by SnazzyDecal (etsy.com); wooden apothecary chest (eBay.com); seagrass storage baskets (amazon.com)

THE ROOMS INSIDE

Photo 54. Kitchen, "after." The wicker baskets and the apothecary chest prevent clutter. And the interaction between the wood and wicker and the metal elements in the kitchen grounds the room in materials we associate with nature.

Accent tiles: SnazzyDecal (etsy.com)
Walls: Wispy Green by Benjamin Moore
Island: Goodnight Moon by Clare Paint (clare.com)
Cupboard door pulls: JackAccessories (etsy.com)
Cesta rattan counter stool (cb2.com)
Seagrass wicker baskets with lids (amazon.com)
Striped cutting board: Handmade by my brother

I didn't want to look at a similar display of my own stuff every time I walked through the door, so I decided to head off the problem. I organized the items I needed into wicker storage baskets with lids and in a vintage wooden apothecary chest I'd found on eBay. The

DESIGN FOR YOUR MIND · 99

Photo 55. Kitchen, "after." Mounting a towel bar on the short side of the island helps keep rumpled dish towels out of sight.

From left: Rustic brass towel bar (nickeykehoe.com); white cutting board, Farberware extra-large plastic cutting board; wooden cutting board, Miyoko's Creamery (miyokos.com); Homaxy 100 percent cotton waffle-weave kitchen dish towels; metal shower curtain hooks

storage baskets now hold duct tape, a pencil, a hammer, and other things I like to keep handy as I work on the house. I use the little drawers in the vintage chest for binder clips, paper clips, rubber bands, and nails. I'm happy to have them separated and not engaged in unsightly comingling in a junk tray.

I placed dividers in the kitchen drawers, so I can store utensils out of sight and find them when I need them. Inside a drawer in the island, I put a clear acrylic rack for storing spice jars.

Remember that studies show that an uncluttered environment reduces our stress and helps us focus on what's important with a clear mind. Not only that, but the very act of decluttering helps reduce stress because the process helps us gain a sense of control.[75] So it's therapeutic to sort through those junk trays and sort the binder clips and rubber bands into little apothecary drawers. And we receive the benefits long before we achieve the finished result.

Along the right-hand side of the island, I mounted an antique brass towel bar. I hang dish towels on it, and I like having the dish towels out of sight from the entrance. I added S-shaped hooks, so I could also hang cutting boards and pans I use often. I store the mixing bowls, colander, and other tools I cook with every day in two cupboards and two drawers near the island. I don't have to walk around the kitchen to fetch them, and when guests help, storing those items in one convenient area makes them easy to find.

PENDANT LIGHTS FOR PERSONALITY

To add more life to the kitchen, I chose two pendant light fixtures in antique brass to hang over the island, and I contacted an electrician recommended by members of my neighborhood Facebook group. I planned to have the fixtures installed with a dimmer switch, so I could create a private getaway when I put on music and could lose myself in my inexpert culinary creations.

75   "Why Decluttering Can Lead to Increased Brain Power," *Psychology Today*

THE ROOMS INSIDE

Photo 56. Kitchen, "after." When hanging lights over a kitchen island, counter, table, or bar, it's best to hang them thirty to thirty-two inches above the surface. Those sitting or standing around will be able to see across the space comfortably. And, when hanging more than one pendant, space the fixtures between twenty-four and thirty-six inches away from each other.

Pendant lamps: Savoy House Alden one-light in warm brass
See "Kitchen Island Pendant Lighting Size Guide," Lightopia

When the electrician arrived, he said he had installed most of the electrical systems in the house decades before. He told me what he knew of the history of the house, mentioning that, as a boy, he had come to know the contractor and tradespeople who had worked on it in the early 1960s. It turns out the homeowners had wanted to update the look and had hired the contractor to demolish the second floor. It was then that the atrium with its towering ceiling was built, and the house was converted from two stories to one. The workers in the 1960s had told my electrician they still remembered the owners' daughters dancing to Beatles songs playing on their record player.

I suspect the owner-wife in the 1960s was the same woman who commissioned the upholstery for the barrel-back chair I found in the basement and whose meticulous taste set the standard for much of the detailed work that still survives in beautiful condition. I hear she was a lovely person.

So, by sheer coincidence, the mystery of the oversized portico and columns was solved. The house had originally been designed to be much taller, and the portico and columns had been drafted to the scale of the house when it was built.

THE BREAKFAST NOOK

The kitchen has a built-in nook surrounded by bay windows—perfect for a round breakfast table. I looked for a table with a fluted pedestal in warm, natural wood tones to create the look of vintage tambour. Tambour was a staple of mid-century modern design. It's the flexible sheet composed of closely set wood strips attached to a piece of cloth that we see used as the cover in a rolltop desk, for example.

In a kitchen, tambour might be used as a flexible door to cover the "garage" area where a standing mixer or a toaster is stored. The flexible tambour sheet slides in grooves along the sides or at the top and bottom of the covered area. I wanted to see the tambour look on the pedestal of a kitchen table.

Photo 57 shows a tambour-look pedestal table I found online. The fluted dowels add texture, the natural wood tones add warmth, and the table brings a mid-century modern vibe. Fluted tambour panels are also available online and at building supply stores. If you go the DIY route, you will find good videos online that show you how to build a fluted pedestal, and you can get the tambour look on a budget by gluing half-round dowels directly to the large cylinder that is designated as the pedestal.

Photo 57. Kitchen, "after." The fluted wood pedestal table, the wicker chairs, and the other natural materials in the kitchen soothe the eye.

Gilta round dining table (wayfair.com)
Barrel-back chairs (target.com)
Serving bowl by Williams Sonoma (eBay.com)

I found the barrel-back wicker chairs at Target. They are sturdy and comfortable, and the rounded backs fit well with the shape of the table and the nook.

I love my new kitchen. I am thrilled that we were able to give it a whole new look by making simple and budget-friendly improvements ourselves. And we sidestepped the long and intrusive disruption we might have expected with a larger kitchen remodeling project.

BRINGING THE FOUR-POSTER BEDROOM TO LIFE

Beyond the atrium is a large room that we call the four-poster bedroom. Despite its special features—a four-poster rope canopy bed left behind by the previous owner, a fireplace with a marble mantel, an antique Italian tole chandelier,[76] a grandfather clock, a high ceiling with intricate crown molding, white embossed wallpaper in good condition, two closets, and a bay window—nothing much had been done with it. After my parents had moved in, the room was used to store orphaned furniture and rugs, board games, and toys the grandchildren had outgrown.

Because the room had not been given much attention since before my parents had bought the house in the late 1990s, I tested any paint that had chipped from the trim for lead. I used disposable, nonstaining lead detection swabs from LeadCheck and ran the test several times. All of the results indicated that the trim paint was lead-free.

BALANCING THE FORMAL FEATURES WITH CASUAL RUGS

The classic features make the room feel formal and old-fashioned. I love them, but I wanted to balance them with details that coax the room to let its hair down. So, after my sister and I sent the rugs and orphaned furniture to the auctioneer, I laid down a large, natural-colored jute rug with a fringe. I chose the rug for the online reviews that commented on its kindness to bare feet. The texture is nubby, and the room felt more casual and fun. Over the jute rug, I laid a red wool area rug handmade in Afghanistan. I found it on Etsy.

---

76   Tole chandeliers are light fixtures made of metal and painted with enamel paint or lacquer. Vintage tole chandeliers trace back to Europe in the 1920s (specifically Florence, Italy), and later were exported around the globe. They're decorated with colorful vines, green leaves, and either porcelain roses or metal flowers.

THE ROOMS INSIDE

Photo 58. Four-poster bedroom, "after." At the foot of the bed is an antique wooden chest that my father brought back from Korea.

*Clockwise from left: Canvas art, Hollywood Blvd by Erin Ashley (greatbigcanvas.com);
mid-century modern chest (anthropologie.com);
table lamp on left, Blair twenty-four-inch table lamp by Birch Lane;
pleated lampshades, large box pleat Empire lampshade (Springcrest);
canvas art over the bed, Portrait of the Countess Nathalie Golovine
by Élisabeth Louise Vigée Le Brun (greatbigcanvas.com);
scalloped bedspread, Brandream white quilts set coverlet;
Roostery duvet cover and pillow shams (spoonflower.com);
mattress, Leesa Sapira hybrid mattress, queen (leesa.com);
I purchased the table lamp on the right-hand side of the bed from an antiques store.
Jute rug: NuLOOM Ashli solid farmhouse jute area rug, ten-by-thirteen, natural
Area rug: Red five-by-seven Gabbeh area rug, Afghan handknotted wool rug by YildizRugs (etsy.com)
Curtains: Ikat blue printed cotton curtain (halfpricedrapes.com)*

ARTWORK THAT INSPIRES

For artwork, I chose a long, narrow modern painting on canvas by Erin Ashley to hang over a two-drawer chest. Over the bed, I hung a classic portrait dating from the late 1700s by a French artist named Élisabeth Louise Vigée Le Brun. Vigée Le Brun was a force; she captured the vibrance and personality of her subjects, and often rendered them in casual poses and garb. Queen Marie Antoinette chose her as her official portrait artist, and in one of the paintings Vigée Le Brun displayed in her salon, the artist scandalized the French court by depicting the monarch in a simple muslin dress and straw hat. Also shocking was

Photo 59. The countess looks happy and relaxed. What a warm smile.

Portrait of the Countess Nathalie Golovine by Élisabeth Louise Vigée Le Brun (greatbigcanvas.com)

Photo 60. Four-poster bedroom, "after." The mid-century modern chest and the modern art give the room a contemporary feel.

Canvas art: Hollywood Blvd by Erin Ashley (greatbigcanvas.com)
Mid-century modern two-drawer chest (anthropologie.com)

Vigée Le Brun's habit of capturing the radiant smiles of her subjects, and in one beaming self-portrait, Vigée Le Brun's smile revealed her own teeth. How vulgar! But, over two hundred years later, Vigée Le Brun's portraits glow with a love of life.

I chose the *Portrait of Countess Nathalie Golovine* because of Vigée Le Brun's artistry, the joy the work inspires in me, and the artist's sheer iconoclasm and cheek. She and the countess are welcome in my home.

Photo 61. Four-poster bedroom, "after." I chose the pleated lampshade for its soothing Empire shape and texture.

Table lamp: Blair twenty-four-inch table lamp by Birch Lane
Pleated shade: Large box pleat Empire lampshade (Springcrest)
Ingram three-drawer nightstand in indigo (anthropologie.com)

Photo 62A.

CURTAINS: CUSTOM-MADE QUALITY FOR HALF THE PRICE

The ikat printed cotton curtains were a find. I ordered them online from a company called Half Price Drapes.[77] They arrived within days, and they have the look and feel of custom-made curtains. The fabric is high-quality, and the curtains are lined. And, as you may have guessed from the company's name, the price was very reasonable.

The company provided custom-made quality and workmanship with careful attention to detail, while sparing me the wait for a custom order and without stretching my budget. I am one happy customer.

77 Half Price Drapes. https://www.halfpricedrapes.com/

THE ROOMS INSIDE

Photo 62B. Four-poster bedroom, "after." The bold design of the ikat printed cotton curtains is echoed on a smaller scale in the printed quilt at the foot of the bed.

*Roostery duvet cover (spoonflower.com)
Ikat blue damask printed cotton custom curtains (halfpricedrapes.com)*

DESIGN FOR YOUR MIND · 111

SLEEP!

Designing a bedroom for our minds means more than creating a beautiful space. It also means creating a refuge where we can find the uninterrupted sleep we need to keep our brains healthy. During sleep, we repair and grow our brains, process what we have learned, consolidate memories, and restore our bodies. In later life, quality sleep promotes general health and adaptability. It's essential to successful growth and successful aging. A good night's sleep also helps us engage with life during the day, when we can take advantage of other activities that protect our brain health.[78] And sleep is also essential to our mental health.[79]

In the footnote below, you'll find tips to help you get a good night's sleep.[80] As the article points out, keeping our rooms cool, dark, and quiet is key, and you can focus on these features in your design. You can choose bedding that's cushy but keeps you from overheating. You can choose a mattress that helps you relax and sleep soundly, so you're not thrashing about all night in search of a comfortable position or waking up at three in the morning.[81] You can choose a weighted blanket that will provide comfort with its gentle pressure.[82] You can block light with room-darkening shades and blackout curtains. Those curtains, rugs, and upholstered furniture also dampen noise because they absorb sound. A bookcase installed against a wall dampens sound that comes through the wall.

---

78 "Environmental Factors Promoting Neural Plasticity: Insights from Animal and Human Studies - PMC," *PubMed Central*

79 "Understanding the Connection Between Sleep and Mental Health," *Psychology Today*

80 "Sleep tips: 6 steps to better sleep," *Mayo Clinic*

81 I chose the Leesa Sapira hybrid mattress to replace the decades-old firm mattress I inherited with the four-poster bed. Later, when we discuss renovations to the bedrooms in the guesthouse, I'll tell you why I chose that mattress. Leesa Sapira hybrid mattress with memory foam and individually wrapped springs, https://www.leesa.com/products/leesa-hybrid-mattress

82 "4 Top Weighted Blankets Benefits, According to Experts," *Good Housekeeping*

You have probably discovered already that sticking to a regular bedtime, not eating before bed, keeping your bed free of clutter, and turning off blue light help you sleep through the night.

My epiphany occurred when I discovered that not watching disturbing movies or reading heartbreaking news stories late at night made a big difference to my sleep, although why it took me so long to figure this out has yet to reveal itself. Now, if I watch a movie before bed, I look for something funny and smart, made with a generous spirit. I sleep better when I have hope for the world.

MAKING ROOM FOR EXERCISE

Where I live, winters are achingly beautiful, but they are also long and cold with short, dark days and icy roads. I didn't want to miss out on regular aerobic exercise for months every year, so I had to find a place in the house for my favorite exercise equipment. It had to be a place I wanted to be—a room that stays warm in the winter and looks and feels comforting and fun. Otherwise, I would find excuses to avoid it and my daily workouts.

The solution was my bedroom. My early-model AB Doer abdominal trainer and my Thigh-Master and rowing machine don't take up a lot of space, and they don't detract from the look of the room with garish colors. First thing in the morning, I can listen to my playlist on Spotify and get in a good workout, even in the dark or during a storm.

Why is this important? We all need aerobic exercise to maintain brain health throughout our lives. According to David J. Linden, PhD, a professor of neuroscience at Johns Hopkins University in Baltimore, not only does aerobic exercise send blood to the brain; regular aerobic exercise can also stimulate the growth of new blood vessels. Aerobic exercise can even stimulate the brain to produce new cells through a process called neurogenesis, leading to an overall improvement in brain performance and helping prevent cognitive

Photo 63. Four-poster bedroom, "after." The subtle colors and classic design of the early-model AB Doer blend into my bedroom. I found mine in perfect pre-owned condition on eBay.

AB Doer twist abdominal trainer by Thane Fitness (eBay.com)
ThighMaster (amazon.com)
Blue mid-century armchair: Amelia 25.6-inch wide side chair by Etta Avenue

decline.[83] As Linden says, regular exercise is "the single best thing one can do to slow the cognitive decline that accompanies normal aging."[84]

83 "The Truth Behind 'Runner's High' and Other Mental Benefits of Running" *Johns Hopkins Medicine*

84 Ibid., 2.

But there's more. You might know that regular exercise can relieve mild to moderate depression. One reason is that it stimulates nerve cell growth in the hippocampus, a part of the brain that regulates emotions. That strengthens nerve cell connections and increases the hippocampus's volume.[85] The hippocampus is also the part of the brain associated with memory and learning, so regular exercise helps build cognitive strength as it relieves depression.[86]

The immediate mood-altering effects are also a kick. Aerobic exercise stimulates the brain to produce endocannabinoids—biochemical substances similar to cannabis, but naturally produced by the body.[87] For years, we've attributed the "runner's high" to the release of endorphins, a group of hormones responsible for numbing pain, among other benefits. But further research shows that endorphins are not likely to be responsible because they don't cross the blood-brain barrier. Endocannabinoids do, however, and they cross it freely. We should probably thank endocannabinoids then, and not endorphins, for our post-exercise high. Endocannabinoids also reduce anxiety and promote feelings of calm.[88] Given all the benefits of exercise, it makes sense to make room for it when we design for our minds.

---

85 "Exercise is an all-natural treatment to fight depression," *Harvard Health*
86 "The Truth Behind 'Runner's High' and Other Mental Benefits of Running," *Johns Hopkins Medicine*
87 Ibid., 1.
88 Ibid., 2.

Photo 64. Four-poster bathroom, "before." Placing two patterns beside each other can be tricky, as you can see here with the patterned cultured marble and the patterned wallpaper. The eye does not focus on the beauty of either design element.

THE RIDDLE OF THE FOUR-POSTER BATHROOM

The bathroom next to the four-poster bedroom presented me with choices. A previous owner had installed cultured marble in a white, gray, and taupe pattern on the countertops, in the shower stall, and surrounding the bathtub. The marble is beautiful and still in good condition.

The same owner also hung vinyl wallpaper with a gold-and-white pattern—again, elegant and in good condition. But the pattern in the cultured marble and the pattern in the wallpaper were waging a quiet war, and one of them had to go. I decided to remove the wallpaper, prep and paint the walls, and keep the marble.

I thought removing the wallpaper would be the easier job, but I had yet to discover the extraordinary tenacity of the wallpaper adhesive used half a century ago. The photo above shows the marble and wallpaper combination "before."

THE *CLEOPATRA* TUB IS A KEEPER. BUT THE WALLPAPER WANTS TO STICK AROUND, TOO.

You'll notice the sunken bathtub. These tubs seized the popular imagination in the 1960s and 1970s, inspired by a fascination with ancient cultures and with the Elizabeth Taylor-Richard Burton epic *Cleopatra*, released in 1963. The cultured marble that surrounds the tub was probably installed in the 1960s or 1970s, and the wallpaper was chosen at that time to enhance the luxurious vibe.

That the wallpaper remained intact in the steamy environment of a bathroom over fifty years later might give you an idea of the strength of the adhesive used for the job. Figuring out how to remove it and prep the walls for painting would have challenged Pythagoras. Because any trace of adhesive would interact with the new paint and spoil the finish, we knew we would have to sand the walls after the adhesive was removed, and then seal them with a special product before we could begin painting.

But, as it turned out, the job was bigger than that. I will take you through the steps we followed in case you, too, plan to remove decades-old wallpaper in a bathroom. This process may save you precious time and effort.

REMOVING THAT DECADES-OLD WALLPAPER

First, we removed the vinyl wallpaper with a heat gun.[89] We didn't use the steamer for this job because we didn't want to risk damaging the old drywall with moisture. Then we tried to remove the adhesive with two products that we knew to be effective on modern-day wallpaper adhesive. But they had no effect on this old-style adhesive. So we went back with

---

89 Because the wallpaper was vinyl, we could use a heat gun to remove it. If the wallpaper had been paper, the heat gun would have caused the wallpaper to burn.

the heat gun and used it directly on the walls to soften the adhesive some more, and we removed it with a wallpaper scraper.

We weren't surprised to find mold. The products available now to help prevent its growth under wallpaper in bathrooms weren't available fifty years ago. To kill the mold, we applied Home Armor mildew stain remover. We then cut out the areas of drywall that had decayed and used a product called DAP Fast'N Final lightweight spackling to patch them. We used a power sander to remove the remaining adhesive and make the surface smooth. We caulked where necessary, and then went back at the walls with the power sander.

Next, we vacuumed and wiped the walls clean with a solution of trisodium phosphate (TCP)[90] and water to remove all traces of the sanding dust. After that, we applied two coats of Zinsser mold-killing primer, which is formulated to prevent mold growth in bathrooms and other high-humidity environments.

PAINTING THE WALLS

Finally, came the "easy" part: painting the walls. I chose a color from a Benjamin Moore line called Aura Bath and Spa that's made for high-humidity environments. It's resistant to mildew and moisture and can stand up to repeated washings with no color rub-off. I chose Bath Salts, a dusty green-blue that has just enough gray to acknowledge the formal features: the sunken bathtub, the ornate wall sconce, and the brass fixtures. The color also brightens the room, moving it into this millennium.

I chose a semigloss finish to make the paint even more moisture-resistant and to add some of the glamour that was lost when we removed the wallpaper. We gave the walls two coats of Bath Salts, and we applied Whipped by Clare Paint for the trim and cupboards below the two sinks.

---

90   Trisodium phosphate (TCP) is a heavy-duty, all-purpose cleaner used to control paint dust and prepare surfaces for painting.

Photo 65. Four-poster bathroom, "before." Because the bathroom receives no direct sunlight, it's important to use the walls to brighten the room. That is not happening here.

TURNING THE JETTED BATHTUB INTO A SOAKING TUB

As you'll notice in Photo 65, the sunken bathtub features water jets along the inside walls. Jetted bathtubs, also known as whirlpool tubs, burst onto the market in the late 1960s and became the in thing for the next decade or so. The tubs are designed to turn bathing into a therapeutic, spa-like experience by relaxing muscles with water-powered massages. Jets are built into the walls of the tub, and a motor drives water through interior pipes into the jets to deliver the experience.

Jetted tubs require regular and specific maintenance. Without it, the water jets and the pipes that connect to them can become pockets of corrosion, rust, soap scum, bacteria, and

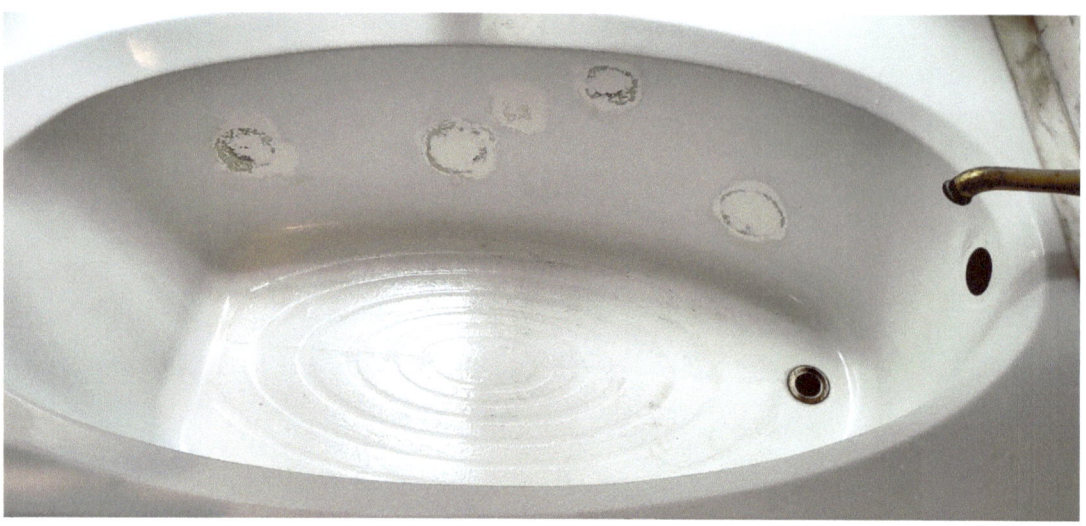

Photo 65A. Jetted bathtub, "in progress."

mold.[91] When I came across this information, I wondered what might be lurking in the jets and the interior pipes in my sunken tub and about the condition of the motor. The tub had been installed half a century ago, and I knew it hadn't been used or maintained in years.

I prefer simple and low-maintenance to fancy and fussy, and I wanted to avoid the costs that using and maintaining a jetted tub would entail. So my decision was easy. But, rather than remove the jetted tub and install a new one without jets, I looked for ways to convert the tub I had.

My local plumber recommended a small business that refinishes old bathtubs. The owner told me his company had long experience converting old jetted tubs to nonmotorized soaking tubs, and the price he quoted was a fraction of what I would have paid for a new tub.

After Kurt disconnected the wires from the motor and taped them off, a two-person team from the company removed the jets and the intake port and covered the openings with

---

91 "Microbial Loads in Whirlpool Baths," *PM Engineer*
See also: "Whirlpool baths: enter at your own risk," *NBC News*

Photo 65B. Jetted bathtub, "after conversion."

The new surface of the tub cured over the next two days. The faucet was wrapped to prevent drips into the tub before the curing process was complete.

resin and fiberglass mats. Then they skimmed the patched areas using 3M Bondo putty with a hardener and sanded them.

Finally, the team refinished the tub with acrylic and a hardener. The workers knew the process and the products well, and they wore respirators as they worked. The work was completed in less than a day, and my vintage sunken tub looks like new. It's now a luxurious, deep soaking tub that's low-maintenance and safe to enjoy.

THE BATHROOM IS JUST THE PLACE FOR A WASHABLE RUG

I took another step to brighten the room with a rug by Annie Selke with an elegant tile pattern on a warm taupe background. Like the paint color, the rug nods to the formal features of the bathroom, but the black accents make it fun. The taupe background is heathered to create the appearance of jute, but unlike jute, the rug is machine washable. It won't spend

Photo 66. Four-poster bathroom, "after."

Towel bar by TimelessDesignWorks (etsy.com)
Wall: Bath Salts by Benjamin Moore, Aura Bath and Spa
Trim: Whipped by Clare Paint (clare.com)

much time in the washing machine, but it's perfect for the wet conditions in a bathroom. I also found a bamboo cabinet that holds all the extras I want to have on hand.

I love my reimagined bathroom. And now, when I bathe in that sunken tub, I feel like a queen.

Photo 67. Four-poster bathroom, "after." The black accents in the Annie Selke rug echo the dark wood of the vanity bench and the black polka dots in the Kate Spade tote on the sink counter.

*Clockwise from left: "Out to Lunch" tote by Kate Spade (eBay.com);
fixtures, CREA widespread bathroom faucet;
towel bar by TimelessDesignWorks (etsy.com)
Wall: Bath Salts by Benjamin Moore, Aura Bath and Spa
Trim and cupboards: Whipped by Clare Paint (clare.com)*

Photo 68. The study, "before." The grayish-green walls don't highlight the beauty of the walnut molding, and they make the room look dreary.

SOFTENING THE STUDY

The study has a high ceiling and dark walnut molding along the walls. The walls were painted a somber grayish green. When combined with the dark wood furniture, the molding against the grayish-green walls made the room look heavy and oh-so-serious. I did

THE ROOMS INSIDE

Photo 69. The study, "after." The ivory bouclé armchair adds a mid-century modern touch, and it makes for luxurious comfort as a desk chair.

Clockwise from left: Horse sculpture, Deco 79 polystone horse prancing sculpture; wicker basket, two pieces seagrass baskets with lid by Cunhill;
table lamp from an antiques store
Curtains: Emery linen matte grommet blackout curtain (potterybarn.com)
Walls: Pink Essence by Benjamin Moore
Rug: Jocelyn JOC-06 area rug by Loloi II Rugs (rugs-direct.com)
Chair: Amelia 25.6-inch wide side chair by Etta Avenue

DESIGN FOR YOUR MIND · 125

Photo 70. The study, "after." The throw pillow is pink, but the rough texture of the mudcloth fabric and the faded cerise tones in the pink make the pillow pretty but sophisticated.

Saybrook swivel chair (grandinroad.com)
Pink mudcloth throw pillow by Krinto (etsy.com)

not want to lighten the color of the molding by painting it. The walnut is beautiful; it just needed to be balanced with elements that soften the mood.

To balance the heavy tone of the dark wood with a soft touch, I painted the walls a pale, dusty pink called Pink Essence by Benjamin Moore. As you see in Photo 69, the pink is subtle and not prissy. In fact, in low light, the pink casts only a warm glow and is barely visible.

I added a pink patterned rug I found on rugs-direct.com that's made to stand up to high-traffic areas.[92] I love the feature on the Rugs Direct website that allows visitors to upload photos of a room and virtually audition any number of rugs.[93] I added a large

92 Rugs Direct https://www.rugs-direct.com/
93 Rugs.com is another rug company that lets the customer upload photos of rooms in their home and audition rugs on the website. https://rugs.com/

pink color-block painting by Erin Ashley and a wicker armchair with a pink mudcloth throw pillow.

The study houses my computer printer, my file cabinets, a bookcase, a paper shredder, and office supplies. The desk is big, the bouclé chair is comfortable, and the big window offers generous natural light. The study has all the features of a well-appointed home office, where many people spend their work lives.

But, as I mentioned earlier, I do my actual work in the den. Given the choice, I would rather spend hours stretched out on that comfortable sectional sofa, feet up, laptop in my lap, than work at a desk, however comfortable the chair might be. Thanks to Wi-Fi, I can send my documents from the den to print in the study.

The Guesthouse

Photo 72. Guesthouse living room, "before." Beautiful workmanship in every detail, but it's time to bring other voices into the conversation.

THE LIVING ROOM: TONING DOWN THE TOILE

When my parents bought the property in the late 1990s, they gave me a tour of the guesthouse. It had been decorated by a previous owner, and I was dazzled when I saw the living room. What a celebration of toile de Jouy!

The walls, sofa, armchair, ottoman, and throw pillows were covered in the same green toile fabric.[94] The work was meticulously done; the pattern on the walls matched the outlet covers, which were also covered in the toile fabric. The carpet was plush, and it was also green. The window treatments were in the balloon style in a contrasting green-and-white striped fabric. I thought the room was elegant and lovely.

---

94 "Toile de Jouy: Everything You Need to Know About the Famous Design," *Architectural Digest*

Photo 73. Guesthouse living room, "before." Notice the cording in the matching toile throw pillows and upholstery. And the toile on the walls is fabric, not wallpaper. I did not have the heart to gut this beautiful work.

Years later, I still respected the fine workmanship and the care that went into designing the living room. But I wanted to tone down the toile and the abundance of green. I did not want to remove the wallpaper that remained in flawless condition, twenty-five years after my first visit, and I couldn't justify removing the carpet because it was also in fine condition. I decided my challenge would be to balance the toile with other elements that complement the pattern but broaden the design palette.

I donated the balloon curtains to a thrift store, and I sent the toile-upholstered armchair and ottoman to the basement until I could decide what to do with them. I replaced them with a mid-century modern armchair in ivory bouclé and a big, embroidered throw pillow

Photo 74. Guesthouse living room, "in progress." I did not buy this rug. I wanted an area rug to distract from the toile-covered walls and sofa without creating a cacophony. The photo is an online "audition" of a rug on Rugs Direct. This wheat-colored jute rug is beautiful, but the wheat color makes the rug too obviously jute to work on a plush carpet. Fortunately, I didn't have to purchase this rug only to find it didn't work. On another note, I thought the manufacturer's lampshade that arrived with the floor lamp needed some texture.

Clockwise from left: Floor lamp, Birthel sixty-two-inch floor lamp by Birch Lane; Gabriola ivory bouclé lounge chair (article.com); embroidered pillow by Pottery Barn from @j_beez (poshmark.com); sculpture on bookshelf, Scotdonadi0 (eBay.com) Rug: Surya jute natural woven, wheat (rugsdirect.com)

from Pottery Barn that I found on Poshmark.[95] The pillow was a find. The flash of red and the embroidered texture draw the eye to the diagonal corner. I placed a bold, mid-century modern floor lamp beside the ivory armchair, and on the bookcase shelf behind the armchair, I put a large clay pot from Egypt that I found on eBay.

95 Poshmark, https://poshmark.com/

My intent was to draw people's eyes to the floor lamp, armchair, embroidered throw pillow, and the mantel area when they enter the room.

THE LONG SEARCH FOR THE RIGHT RUG

Finding the right area rug to cover the green carpet was a challenge. I wanted to distract the eye from the green toile on the walls and the sofa without creating a cacophony by using a rug that would scream for attention and compete with the toile. A plain-colored rug without texture would not have distracted from the toile, and a brightly colored rug or one with a distinctive pattern would have created too much noise. I saw my choices as between a rug with a subtle pattern and a rug with texture and subtle variations within a single color.

Again, I used the preview feature on the Rugs Direct website. Seeing how each rug played with the toile wallpaper and upholstered sofa was essential because I was pursuing a specific design goal. Auditioning rugs online also spared me some of the frustration and expense of laying down a rug, only to find it did not work.

After a long search, I found my winner—on clearance. It's a jute rug in a greenish-gray heathered color created by blending different colored fibers into one piece to create a multicolored effect. The heathering and the texture draw the eye quietly, and the warm color makes the room feel cozy. It also gives the jute a dressier look than jute in a tan shade and makes it compatible with the plush green carpet. As a bonus, the rug is soft underfoot.[96]

I thought the manufacturer's lampshade that arrived with the floor lamp needed some texture.

---

96 Rugs Direct, https://www.rugs-direct.com/

Photo 75. Lampshade, "after." The lampshade after I gave it faux pleats using ivory linen frayed fringe ribbon and a glue gun. To create the faux pleats, I wrapped ribbon around the lampshade and allowed for a quarter-inch overlap with each wrap. I could do this without creating a fire hazard because the wide drum shape keeps the inside surface of the shade a safe distance from the light bulb. For a narrower lamp, I would cut individual pleats and apply each one to the outside of the shade with a glue gun. The rug is the greenish-gray one I purchased from the Rugs Direct website.

Ribbon: Keypan ivory ribbon, 1½ x 15 yards, handmade cotton frayed fringe fabric ribbons

THE GUESTHOUSE

Photo 76. Living room, "in progress." Getting there, but the mantel needs an arrangement that will draw the eye to the far wall, so it can take more attention from the toile walls and sofa. The embroidered throw pillow on the bouclé armchair is sold at Pottery Barn, but I purchased it new from Poshmark, an online site that lets individuals sell directly to buyers. The embroidered texture adds beauty and interest and makes the pillow special, and it was a bargain.

GOING BIG WITH THE MANTEL

The photo above shows the living room before I arranged the mantel area. I had made a lot of changes, but I wasn't quite there yet.

My goal for the mantel in the living room of the guesthouse was different from my goal for the mantel in the atrium and the den of the main house. Here, I wanted the mantel to be the star because I wanted to use it to draw the eye to the diagonal corner and the far wall

THE GUESTHOUSE

Photo 77. Guesthouse living room, "after." I think we've got it now. The corner and mantel area offer a variety of eye-catching shapes, textures, and colors, yet the objects coordinate well with one another. The eye registers more than green and green toile when it takes in the room.

Clockwise from left:. Birthel sixty-two-inch floor lamp by Birch Lane (I added faux pleats to the lampshade with cotton frayed-edge ribbon); armchair, Gabriola ivory bouclé lounge chair (article.com); embroidered pillow on armchair by Pottery Barn from @j_beez (poshmark.com) On the bookcase: Large clay pot from Egypt from corky00 (eBay.com) On mantel: Fourteen-inch preserved boxwood topiary in pot by Charlton Home (wayfair.com); iron taper candle holders in antique brass; framed etching from a thrift shop On sofa: Pommed jute pillows (anthropologie.com) Rug: Surya jute natural woven, light gray (rugsdirect.com)

to take in the toile but not be run over by it. Again, I used a large mirror as an anchor and arranged pieces in different shapes, colors, and textures on either side.

But this time, I layered liberally to create depth and interest. I positioned three brass candlesticks of different heights in front of the mirror and the framed etching well into its area. The odd number of candlesticks and their different heights draw focus. But, again, I kept things asymmetrical by placing more objects on the left-hand side of the mantel than on the right-hand side.

And, as you see on the opposite page, I added more drama with the little boxwood topiary to the left of the candlesticks that's perched on two hardcover books to give it more height. The topiary balls echo the cylindrical features of the standing lamp, the rounded shape of the clay pot, and the round shapes in the design of the throw pillow on the armchair. The weight on each side of the mantel is even because the framed etching on the right-hand side is a decent size. Here's the result below.

Now when I stand in the doorway and look into the living room, my eye is drawn to the corner with the armchair, and I take in the standing lamp with the faux-pleated lampshade, the armchair, the throw pillow, the clay pot, and all the objects on the mantel. My eye is no longer overwhelmed by the toile, and the room finds some balance.

This redesign was a good exercise because it coaxed me to find ways to accept what I had elected not to change—the toile-covered walls and the green carpet—and to work with what I had. In the psychology world, that is known as *radical acceptance.*[97] I'm finding it's a skill that comes in handy—even in design.

---

97   *Radical acceptance* is a skill that clients learn to help them cope with strong emotions through a type of cognitive behavior therapy called dialectical behavior therapy (DBT). "Dialectical Behavior Therapy (DBT): What It Is & Purpose," *Cleveland Clinic*

Photo 78. Guesthouse big bedroom, "before." For the walls, I chose On Point by Clare Paint. It's the color on the swatch at the top left.

THE BEDROOMS

The two bedrooms presented a different challenge. Both rooms had twin beds with mattresses that my visiting brother gently reported had never been all that comfortable. Unlike the living room challenge, the bedrooms were all mine. I could start with a clean canvas.

I wanted to create a space in both that made my guests feel relaxed, at home, and pampered. I also wanted the rooms to be stimulating but not agitating, and peaceful but not boring.

THE BIG BEDROOM: CREATING A QUIET SPACE

I started with the larger bedroom. As I had done with the rooms in the main house, I aimed to create a space that was not tied to a particular period or place. I began with the walls, choosing the same warm taupe I'd used in the guest bathroom and foyer in the main house: On Point by Clare Paint. And I used the same warm off-white for the trim: Whipped by Clare Paint.

To bring a feeling of airiness, I chose white textured curtains with grommets.[98] They are light-filtering but not blackout. I gravitate to texture to give a room warmth and interest, and the square embellishments in the pattern echo at a smaller scale in the squares of the white waffle-weave duvet cover, also textured, that I chose for the king-size bed. Ah, fractals!

I wanted to create a soothing feel in the room, using natural elements, textures, and colors. I chose Roman window shades in a warm, natural bamboo that are light-filtering but not blackout. The shades offer privacy, and they also shield guests from the morning sun as it shines in through the two east-facing windows, allowing them to sleep. I ordered the custom Roman shades online. The manufacturer, LANTIME, had received enthusiastic customer reviews, and the website gave clear instructions for measuring my windows to ensure a perfect fit. Installing the shades took only a few minutes.[99]

Rehoming a bed is a challenge. Many nonprofits will not accept used mattresses, box springs or, or even headboards. I gave the twin mattresses in the larger bedroom to a friend who owns a pet resort. The mattresses are now enjoyed by large dogs. And finally, I found a local nonprofit that would accept the box springs and bed frames. The nonprofit, which makes furniture available at no charge to families who need it, picked them up for a small fee.

Then I researched beds and chose a mid-century modern wood frame made by Thuma.[100] Putting it together was fun. No tools required! Each piece slotted together neatly, like the

---

98   If your room has baseboard heating, as this bedroom does, make sure your curtains hang eight to ten inches above the baseboard (and/or at least three inches in front of the baseboard) to ensure proper air circulation. If you need to shorten the curtains to a proper length and don't want to sew by hand, iron-on tape made for hemming is a good option.

99   LANTIME wood window Roman shades, bamboo (m.shein.com)

100 Walnut king bed with pillow board, Thuma, https://www.thuma.co/products/the-bed

Lincoln Logs we used to play with. I also ordered a padded headboard from Thuma that is covered in a light gray fabric.

Then I researched mattresses. Glowing professional and consumer reviews led me to the Leesa Sapira hybrid mattress with coils and memory foam.[101] It's designed to accommodate whatever sleeping positions my guests favor, whether they're side, back, or face-down

---

101   Leesa Sapira hybrid mattress with memory foam and individually wrapped springs, https://www.leesa.com/products/leesa-hybrid-mattress

THE GUESTHOUSE

PREVIOUS PAGE: **Photo 79. Guesthouse big bedroom, "after."** I chose blues, greens, textures, and natural tones to make my guests feel relaxed and at home. The pom-pom blanket was handmade at an Etsy shop in Morocco. Photo: Taylor B. Cartwright

Mirror: Clavie decorative round mirror, twenty-four-inch
Walls: On Point by Clare Paint (clare.com)
Trim: Whipped by Clare Paint (clare.com)
Curtains: Squared embellished grommet top curtain panel pair, Exclusive Home (target.com)
Roman shades: LANTIME wood window Roman shades, pattern five (m.shein.com)
Upholstered bench: Avery II upholstery bench (jossandmain.com)
Mirror: G-LEAF black round mirror, twenty-inch
Standing lamp: Braxton arc lamp, dark bronze, Adesso (target.com)
Wicker armchair: Iraan 29.1-inch polyester barrel chair by Dovecove
Throw pillow: Thibaut Corneila pillow, Pillow Fever (etsy.com)
Antique painting of pink chrysanthemum: From my grandmother's estate, brought from Japan by her parents in the early 1900s
King-size bed (thuma.co); Mattress: Leesa Sapira hybrid mattress, king (leesa.com)
Duvet cover: Bedspreads cotton duvet cover set, 100 percent cotton
Waffle weave Moroccan pom-pom blanket by Berber Blanket (etsy.com)
Rug: Safavieh Aspen Collection handmade boho braided tassel wool rug

sleepers. I ordered the mattress online, and once I released it from its shrink-wrapped packaging, I had fun watching it grow to its full size and firmness. My guests say they sleep like babies. And now, so do I. I spent a night on the Leesa Sapira hybrid mattress myself and slept so soundly that I ordered one for the four-poster bed in the main house. I no longer toss and turn. I had no idea a mattress could make such a difference.

Over the king-size bed, I hung an abstract minimalist oil and acrylic painting by a Hong Kong artist I found on Etsy. The painting reflects a *wabi-sabi* approach to design—quiet, intentional, simple, and embracing imperfections.[102] The beige and brown tones are soothing, and they work well with the blues and greens in the room and with the dark-gray, padded headboard.

102 "What Is Wabi Sabi Interior Design? How to Use It at Home," *The Spruce*

Photo 80. Guesthouse big bedroom, "after." This giant throw pillow draws the eye when one enters the room. The pillow was made by one of my favorite Etsy small-business owners.

Wicker armchair: Iraan 29.1-inch polyester barrel chair by Dovecove
Pillow: Thibaut Corneila pillow, Pillow Fever (etsy.com)

I love the way the painting intimates the process of falling asleep. Our initial state of full consciousness can be represented by the beige color in the top section. Then we become drowsy, as represented by the heavier light-brown below. And finally, we fall into slumber, as represented by the dark brown band that runs along the bottom edge of the canvas. The

THE GUESTHOUSE

Photo 81. Guesthouse big bedroom, "after." The beige and brown oil and acrylic painting quietly brings the room together to create a private space where guests can relax and recharge. And the faded areas illustrate the beauty in imperfection.

Avery II upholstery bench (jossandmain.com)
Wicker armchair: Iraan 29.1-inch polyester barrel chair by Dovecove
Throw pillow: Thibaut Corneila pillow, Pillow Fever (etsy.com)
Antique painting of pink chrysanthemum: From my grandmother's estate,
brought from Japan by her parents in the early 1900s
Standing lamp: Braxton arc lamp, dark bronze, Adesso (target.com)
Walls: On Point by Clare Paint (clare.com)
Trim: Whipped in semigloss by Clare Paint (clare.com)
Table lamp in corner: Maggie ceramic table lamp by Kelly Clarkson Home (wayfair.com)
King-size bed (thuma.co)
Mattress: Leesa Sapira hybrid mattress, king (leesa.com)
Duvet cover: Bedspreads cotton duvet cover set, 100 percent cotton, waffle weave
Moroccan pom-pom blanket by Berber Blanket (etsy.com)
Round pillow: Anthropologie embroidered Paola pillow from @meadowlands (poshmark.com)
Lumbar pillow: Thibaut Palampore Bird lumbar pillow in blue by PillowFever (etsy.com)
Painting: Beige wabi-sabi painting, beige brown abstract painting by UniqueartworkByAnne (etsy.com)
Table lamp near door came from my parents' estate
Rug: Safavieh Aspen Collection handmade boho braided tassel wool rug

DESIGN FOR YOUR MIND · 143

Photo 82. Guesthouse big bedroom, "after." The orange accents in the pillow balance the abundance of neutral colors, blues, and greens in the room, and the accents in the pillow pick up the orange accents in the area rug.

Round pillow: Anthropologie embroidered Paola pillow from @meadowlands (poshmark.com)
Lumbar pillow: Thibaut Palampore Bird lumbar pillow in blue by PillowFever (etsy.com)

painting pulls together the colors and elements of the room, while it signals that it is a place where guests can relax and find repose.

The bed needed a round throw pillow to soften the straight lines in the room. I found an exquisite round, embroidered throw pillow by Anthropologie on Poshmark, the same site where I found the embroidered Pottery Barn pillow in the guesthouse living room. Again, I paid a bargain price.

Photo 83. Guesthouse small bedroom, "before." The small bedroom has plenty of natural light.

MAKING THE SMALLER BEDROOM FEEL SPACIOUS

The second bedroom is smaller and sunnier, with windows facing both east and south. To make guests feel they had room to breathe, I chose an icy blue color called Frozen by Clare Paint for the walls. The cool blue makes the small room look larger because it makes the walls appear to recede.[103] That's a special power of cool colors, which are blues, greens, and purples. They register on the brain more slowly than warm colors—which are reds, yellows, and oranges—so cool colors appear to move away from the eye.[104]

---

103 "Understanding Warm Colors and Cool Colors," *The Spruce*
104 "Understanding Color: Temperature," *Charlene Collins Freeman Art*

THE GUESTHOUSE

Photo 84. Guesthouse small bedroom, "after." The cool blue creates breathing room. The wall sconce over the queen-size bed saves space as it provides light. Photo: Taylor B. Cartwright.

Table lamp: Maggie ceramic table lamp by Kelly Clarkson Home;
Lampshade: Large box pleat Empire shade lamp,
Springcrest Walls: Frozen by Clare Paint (clare.com) Trim: Whipped by Clare Paint (clare.com)
Curtains: Squared embellished grommet top curtain panel pair, Exclusive Home (target.com)
Roman shades: LANTIME wood window Roman shades, pattern five (amazon.com)
Upholstered bench: Alpine Furniture Flynn bench (hayneedle.com)
Striped throw blanket: Amazon Aware woven cotton throw striped blanket (amazon.com)
Mirror: Diafline black round mirror
Throw pillow: Authentic African pillow, blue mudcloth by Krinto (etsy.com)
Artwork: La Rotonda di Palmieri by Giovanni Fattori (greatbigcanvas.com)
Queen-size bed (thuma.co)
Mattress: Leesa Sapira hybrid mattress, queen (leesa.com)
Duvet cover: Bedspreads cotton duvet cover set, 100 percent cotton, waffle weave
Lampshade: Large box pleat Empire lampshade, Springcrest

Cool colors are also associated in nature with wide open spaces, strengthening the message I wanted Frozen to deliver.

What's more, any pale color, whether cool or warm, will appear to recede, while a dark color will appear to advance.[105] Frozen, as a pale blue, helped transform the small bedroom into a room that felt large enough for guests to breathe and relax.

In choosing the wall color, I also focused on another feature: the windows facing east and south. The room receives abundant sunlight in the mornings and generous sunlight throughout the day. Because the bedroom is small, and I didn't want my guests to feel overwhelmed by brightness in a confined space, I chose a blue that would keep its cool at any time of day. Although blue is a cool color, it can appear cooler still when it moves in the direction of violet, but warmer in its more yellowish varieties. To make sure the blue stays cool in all light conditions, I chose Frozen, with its subtle violet undertones. Whipped by Clare Paint is perfect for the trim.

I wanted to replace the twin beds and their wooden pineapple frames with a queen-size bed that would give me room to vacuum around it and change the sheets without a struggle. The same nonprofit that took the box springs and the frame from the bigger bedroom picked up the twin beds. I ordered a Thuma bed and a Leesa Sapira hybrid mattress for this bedroom, too.[106] I also chose the same square embellished grommet curtains and the Roman shades and waffle-weave duvet cover that had worked in the larger bedroom.

Because the room is small and a tall dresser would overpower it, I took advantage of the area beneath the east-facing window. I found a mid-century modern upholstered bench with two drawers for that spot. Just the place for guests to store their clothes.

---

105 "Cool Colors Versus Warm Colors in Interior Design," *Eccos Paints*

106 Leesa Sapira hybrid mattress with memory foam and individually wrapped springs, https://www.leesa.com/products/leesa-hybrid-mattress

You may recognize the framed picture in Photo 84 as the same painting by Giovanni Fattori that hangs in the guest bathroom in the main house. I originally ordered the framed picture for the guest bathroom, but I didn't account for the additional size of the frame when I measured for the picture's fit over the bathroom mirror. I realized my mistake when the framed picture arrived. So I hung the framed picture in this bedroom and ordered the picture again without a frame. The unframed canvas fits perfectly in the guest bathroom of the main house, and the framed picture makes a statement in this smaller bedroom. I chose the round mirror with the thick black frame for this smaller bedroom to echo the thick black frame of the picture.

The small bedroom finally looks inviting and not confining, a refuge where a guest can relax and enjoy downtime for naps and reading.

Photo 85. Guesthouse bathroom. I arranged fresh cuttings of blossoming dogwood in one of the many generic glass vases that I have collected over the years and placed the vase inside a wicker basket.

THE BATHROOM

The showerhead in the bathroom only dribbled, but that was an easy fix. We replaced it, and I stocked up on thick white towels and a cushy white bath mat.[107] The wallpaper is a classic; it's Waverly Savoy, a pattern that's hard to find now. It's in good condition, and I'll keep it.

107 Yimobra bath rug mat

Photo 86. Guesthouse kitchen, "before." I had never renovated a galley kitchen before. I went to Pinterest to find the secrets to making one work.

THE GALLEY KITCHEN FINDS ITS GROOVE

The little galley kitchen in the guesthouse was a bit down in the dumps. The appliances were decades old, the cupboards white, and the counters a beige laminate. I needed some ideas to turn a small space into something with personality without making it look crowded and chaotic. The floor space measures only five feet by seven feet, so every decision would count.

REPLACING THE COUNTERTOPS

The first decision I made was to replace the beige laminate countertops. So far, my work in the main house and the guesthouse had been limited to painting and other modest improvements, making the countertops one of my bigger expenses.

WHEN I GOT TO KNOW THAT "DECADES-OLD" REFRIGERATOR, I LEARNED SOME RESPECT. IT'S A GE FROST GUARD, MADE IN THE 1960S. REFRIGERATORS OF THAT ERA OFFERED FEATURES MORE SPACE-AGE THAN ANYTHING WE SEE TODAY. SHELVES REVOLVED AND THEIR HEIGHT COULD BE ADJUSTED WITH THE PUSH OF A BUTTON. BUTTER COULD BE STORED AT ANY TEMPERATURE. THESE OLD GEMS WERE BUILT TO LAST, AND THEY'RE HARD TO FIND TODAY BECAUSE THEY'RE KEEPERS. LESSON HAPPILY LEARNED.

For pricey improvements, I make sure to choose products that are classic and can work with a variety of styles. I like the pure white Corian countertops in the main house kitchen and love that they are still beautiful and in pristine condition some twenty-five years after my mom had them installed.

I gravitated toward white Corian or another plain white product for the guesthouse kitchen, too. I wanted to avoid a pattern that might not work with any changes I'd make to the kitchen down the road. I like to position myself so that I have room to move and breathe, and I want the flexibility to make a different design choice as I'm inspired.

Another benefit of a plain white countertop is that it won't darken the room. And, if I do decide someday to go dark and moody with the cabinets—say, paint them midnight blue—the white countertops will add contrast and drama, making the kitchen look mysterious, not gloomy.

I found a company online called Colors2U.net that sent me samples of Corian products in shades of white,[108] and I ordered samples of other solid-surface countertop materials in white from Home Depot, so I could examine the look and feel of each and appreciate the substantial weight of the materials.

I tapped my community Facebook group for recommendations of a local Corian installer. When I contacted one of the two local Corian installers the group members suggested and sent him diagrams with my measurements, his estimate was much more than I wanted to pay. I sleuthed some more and circled back to Home Depot.

Home Depot sells Corian, HIMACS, and other solid-surface countertop brands, and it coordinates the projects and works with a local third-party contractor who installs them. I completed the initial questionnaire on the company's website, and the countertop coordinator contacted me by phone the next day. I sent her the diagrams I had made for the other installer. She was responsive and personable, and she sent me Home Depot's estimate a day later. It was a fraction of the price that had been submitted by the first business I'd contacted. So I went with Home Depot.

The installer kept me informed at every step in the process and answered my questions promptly. A technician came out to take measurements. The countertop was fabricated at the installer's facility, where the technician said the workers use the proper clothing, masks, ventilation, techniques, and equipment to avoid exposure to the dust created during fabrication. The installation went smoothly, and the countertops were just what I'd wanted.

---

108 "Corian Design Samples," *Colors2U*, https://coriandesignsamples.colors2u.net/

THE GUESTHOUSE

Photo 87. Guesthouse kitchen, "after." I found the glass pieces and the handmade checkered wooden cutting board on eBay. They help bring the kitchen alive.

Clockwise from left: Vidrios San Miguel aqua blue vase, handmade in Spain, from thrifted_attic (eBay.com); MCM chrome yellow glass vase, handblown, from katiestash (eBay.com); Blenko green donut vase with ruffled edge, handblown, from Nln1527 (eBay.com); checkered wooden cutting board, handmade, by 937mas_sales (eBay.com) Walls: Wall tile decal vinyl sticker by Snazzy Decal (etsy.com)

My entire experience with purchasing and installation was perfect. The employees at both companies were professional, personable, and competent, and I appreciated the big cost savings.

LOOKING FOR INSPIRATION

Meanwhile, I scoured Pinterest for ideas for the overall look. The most successful galley kitchens I found used the far wall—whether it's a window, a solid wall, or a distant wall seen through an entrance into an adjoining room—to create a focal point. It was always an interesting object—a piece of art, a window frame painted in a powerful color, or a large object with a distinctive shape. And I noticed that successful galley kitchen designs also led the eye to the focal point with a unique runner or other unusual floor covering, or a line of pendant lamps on the ceiling.

So I looked for ways to add drama to the far wall and the window in the middle of it. Then I looked for ways to lead the eye to the drama.

I decided to paint the white cupboards an energetic blue. I uploaded photos on the Benjamin Moore website and experimented until I found Indi Go-Go—bold, but not so vivid that it would make guests feel like the walls of the tiny kitchen were closing in on them. I chose their Advanced Interior Paint, a line formulated to withstand ordinary wear and tear on kitchen cabinets. To help the paint adhere, we removed the cabinet doors, sanded them lightly, and gave the cabinets two coats of Indi Go-Go.

To add drama to the far wall, I covered it with white vinyl adhesive tiles with tiny black diamond shapes. Then we used the side walls to help lengthen the look of the room and lead the eye to the drama. The trick was to cover the narrow strip of wall above the cupboards and the areas below the cupboards with the same tiles to create two visual runways to the far wall. We painted the window frame Indi Go-Go blue and replaced the old white plastic pull-down window shade with a wicker shade in a natural color. We also removed the beige laminate pop-up countertop that provided extra counter space at the far wall.

I mounted a twelve-inch brass towel bar to the left of the window and hung a paddle-shaped wooden cutting board from a hook on the bar to draw the eye. To make the window more exciting, I chose sheer white curtains with a pom-pom design. I covered the floor with a chunky jute rug to add texture and appeal without competing with the pattern on the walls or the vivid colors in the glass vases and the checkered cutting board on the countertop.

I love glass. It reflects light, and colored glass adds vibrancy. Glass is translucent, so light passes through it. Glass brightens and lightens the look of a room and, I hope, the mood of anyone in the room. I found these preowned glass pieces on eBay, so I'm supporting individuals and small businesses and giving these objects a new home as I save money.

I'm drawn to handblown pieces made at the Blenko Glass Company in Milton, West Virginia, and signed pieces made in Murano, the world-famous islands in the Venetian Lagoon where the art of glassmaking has been perfected and passed down since the late 1200s.

A FUNKY PLANT AS A FOCAL POINT

The structure of a galley kitchen sets the eye up for a big payoff at the far wall, but the kitchen still needed something in front of the window that would catch the eye and fascinate. I wanted a tall plant with a weird shape and unusual foliage that I had never seen before. Trendy plants and old favorites we see every day wouldn't do for this spot.

I pictured the plant with the quirkiness and height I wanted, and I went looking for it online. There I found it: a tall faux water lily. I also chose it for its lack of effusive foliage; an abundance of leaves would have overpowered the tiny kitchen. It turned out to be even more delightfully strange in person.

Photo 88. Guesthouse kitchen, "after." The four-headed faux water lily is just the right size to be strange but not scary. I originally ordered a five-headed water lily that was a foot taller. But the five-headed plant loomed over this tiny galley kitchen and took me back to the man-eating plant in the original version of *Little Shop of Horrors* (1960), a childhood viewing experience I remember to this day. So I moved Audrey Jr. to the large atrium in the main house, where the plant poses no threat, and replaced it with this four-headed, four-foot plant. One must consider the houseguests.

Plant: Waoops artificial trees, faux water lilies with four heads in pot, 4.6 feet
Belly basket: LiloCraft seagrass plant basket, XXL

I placed it in front of the window in a giant seagrass belly basket, where the water lily packed a lot of drama without taking up a lot of space. I chose the belly basket for its rounded shape, natural texture, commanding size, and cute little handles.

Giving the plant the place of honor at the far wall means there is no room for a kitchen trash bin in front of the window. And this galley kitchen is too tiny to accommodate a trash bin anywhere else on the floor. The solution was to hide it in the tall cupboard under the sink. The cupboard allows for a bin measuring no more than eight inches wide and twenty inches deep, but we found a rack and bin that were just the right fit.

The rack we installed now lets us pull the bin out to deposit trash. And, because the rack came with a built-in pull-out handle, we didn't have to remove the hinges from the swinging door to convert it to a pull-out door.[109] There's nothing novel about this setup, but it was crucial to make this small galley kitchen work. Now the trash bin is out of sight, and the focal point of the kitchen is the dramatic water lily plant. Just the payoff I wanted.

The very aspects that had limited the kitchen—its tiny size and fixed layout—turned out to be the features that made it special. Using a variety of textures and shapes created interest; it wasn't necessary to overload the small space with objects. There's now drama at the far wall, and the unbroken line of diamond-patterned tiles above the cupboards on the side walls leads the eye to the drama. The result is a little galley kitchen that's cozy and interesting without feeling confining. The fun, and the reward, came from taking stock of what I had to work with and couldn't change and turning the kitchen's liabilities into its best assets.

---

[109] Knape and Vogt RS-PSW9-1-20-W 17" x 8" steel in-cabinet 20-quart single white pull-out trash can

Photo 89. Guesthouse kitchen, "after." I wanted to make the kitchen feel cozy without overwhelming the small space with unnecessary objects. The textures in the chunky jute rug, pom-pom curtains, wicker belly basket, window shade, glass, and wood add warmth without creating clutter. The square details in the checkered cutting board and curtains accentuate the diamond shapes in the wall tiles but don't compete with them.

PREVIOUS PAGE:
Countertops: HIMACS solid-surface in Arctic White (Home Depot)
Flat cutting board on left: YUSOTAN ebony wood cutting board for kitchen
Walls: Wall tile decal vinyl sticker by Snazzy Decal (etsy.com)
Gas/CO_2 detector: Kidde Nighthawk carbon monoxide detector, propane, natural, methane, and explosive gas alarm (kidde.com)
Brass towel bar: ALOKABRASS (etsy.com)
Round cutting board: Acacia wood cutting board with handle
Curtains: Guken pom-pom sheer white curtains
Window shade: HunterDouglas
Plant: Waoops artificial trees, faux water lilies with four heads in pot, 4.6 feet
Belly basket: LiloCraft seagrass plant basket, XXL
Color lithograph: The Thames Embankment—Looking East, The English School, undated
Rug: Martha Stewart handmade flatweave jute/sisal brown rug by Martha Stewart
Rugs Kitchen cabinets: Benjamin Moore, Advance Interior Paint, Indi Go-Go
Brass cabinet knobs: etsy.com
On righthand countertop: Vintage Blenko crackle vase from upnorthtreasure (eBay.com); MCM chrome yellow glass vase, handblown, from katiestash (eBay.com); Blenko green donut vase with ruffled edge, handblown, from Nln1527 (eBay.com); checkered wooden cutting board, handmade, by 937mas_sales (eBay.com)

WELCOMING GUESTS

I stocked the kitchen with a Keurig coffee maker and a blender for making smoothies. Before my guests arrive, I invite requests. Their favorite coffees and teas, breakfast foods, and snacks are waiting for them, along with the Wi-Fi password for the guesthouse. Privacy and self-sufficiency are treats for my guests and for me. When we're not spending time together, we can have downtime. They can do their thing, as I do mine. After all, that's what a place of our own is all about.

AFTERWORD

As I wrote this book, I would chat about it with people I knew. I was moved to write the book to support family caregivers, but it seems this book speaks to an even broader audience. It turns out that most people I know are facing a new beginning or looking for ways to refresh their home, whether to help support themselves through some challenge or simply to help them recharge and become more productive.

At the hair salon, my stylist told me he was renovating the old house he'd inherited from his grandmother. He struggled to remove the decades-old bathroom wallpaper and said this book would have helped him tackle the old-style adhesive without spending days in trial and error.

I shared my draft with friends and family on Google Docs. My author friend was inspired to paint the inside of her bookshelves with the color I used when she renovated her study. She also decided that the protagonist in the novel she's writing, *Murder at The Naughty Cabbage*, will be reading *Design for Your Mind* as she converts her family home into an inn and spa.

Two friends decided to take action, not only with plans for their own houses, but with the books they've always wanted to publish. My childhood friend and her husband are renovating the galley kitchen at their weekend cabin and are looking for ways to make it work. My niece has used the draft to get ideas for her first apartment. My therapist friends plan to recommend the book to their clients.

All this makes me happy because I wrote this book for people and about people, to help us make design choices that can nurture and make our lives better.

Then shortly before this book was published, I lost my younger brother to cancer. For four years, he had fought, first, to beat the disease. Then after the last remaining treatment option was exhausted, he fought to stay alive for as long as he could because his wife and his children needed him. After he died, his family and friends and I wrestled with questions that will never be answered. My brother was beloved for his paradoxes: He was an extravert who energized people without exhausting them. He had a hundred stories to tell, but he wanted to hear other people's tales. He gave valuable advice, but he'd ask if advice was wanted before he offered it. He was a talented businessman, a natural leader, and a team player. A realist who survived for years against the odds and proved the power of hope. If life was fair, he would have marked every milestone in his children's lives and celebrated another quarter century with his beloved wife.

For a week, my house and the guesthouse and the studio above the garage buzzed with overnight guests who came to town for the funeral services, the dinner, and the reception to celebrate my brother's life. When we ran out of beds, I put guests on plug-in air mattresses with thick quilts and soft pillows. I drew on everything I had learned about loss and resilience from the death of my parents and others I had loved to support my family members and myself. The two years of work to transform the guesthouse and the main house and studio delivered what we needed. The house was warm and welcoming. The beds were comfortable, the rooms were cozy, and guests had the space and privacy they needed for an extended stay. The house and the guesthouse and the studio took care of my grieving family and me at a time when we needed to find solace together and some joy.

Then everyone left. In the quiet, I was gripped by thoughts of mortality. I was numb from the loss of my brother, my parents, and two dear friends within the past year and so ashamed of time I had lost and misspent in my own life that I was afraid I might squander what remained.

Then late one night, I realized that I knew better. I had watched my brother and my two friends fight for every last day with their families, and I remembered one lesson of death. When confronting their mortality in the prime of their lives, my brother and my friends had treated time as a precious gift and welcomed every chance, however slim, to keep it in their hands. Each of them faced their illness with grace and faith, but they battled for the days that remained to them. So I made a choice to honor them and spend my time as purposefully as I spend any other finite resource. Living more fully meant rethinking some habits that were wasting my time and others that were holding me back.

Since then, I've made friends with the butterflies in my stomach when I dare myself to take a risk. I look for opportunities now that scare me a little, that jolt me into the present moment, that demand that I be acutely awake. I'm learning to say, "Yes," or "Why not?" rather than tally the risks and obstacles at the outset and close the door before I set a foot inside. If the opportunity calls for skills I need to polish or develop, or risks or obstacles I must navigate, I trust I'll figure them out. As will you.

Most of our challenges call for executive functioning skills and critical thinking, imagination and resourcefulness, hard work, and determination to follow through. If our years as family caregivers, estate executors, house cleaner-outers, and water carriers in other capacities have left us with anything, it's killer skills in these areas. I've always loved a dark horse, so it thrills me to say this: They'll never see you coming.

I credit this house for what it has given and for what it has taught me. I have learned that some rooms, and some circumstances, call for a fresh start. But when I choose to accept what is, with all its flaws—whether it's a room's structural detail, or a design choice made by a previous owner, an inexplicable loss, or even where the last several years of my life have led me—I can use the friction generated by that reality to ignite new ideas and create something I had not envisioned.

I've learned that the key to accepting loss is to face life, with its kindness and its coldness, its imperfections and impermanence, its revelations, and its unanswered questions. I'm sustained by reminders of family I have loved or never knew, by the thoughtfulness of friends, and by the artistry of people I have never met. And I'm grateful for a home that shelters and cheers me as I meet my next adventure.

I'VE ALWAYS LOVED A DARK HORSE, SO IT THRILLS ME TO SAY THIS: THEY'LL NEVER SEE YOU COMING.

INDEX

A

AB Doer Twist Abdominal Trainer 113, 114

Abstract Expressionist 37, 49

accent tiles 93, 94, 97

accent wall 65, 97

acceptance 6

adventures 6

aerobic exercise xiv, 12, 113, 115

Afghanistan 105

agency 7

air circulation 139

Alzheimers disease 10

Annie Selke rug 121, 123

Anthropologie 82, 106, 108, 109, 136, 144

antique brass towel bar 101

antique bronze pull rings 73

antiques 15, 50

antique slant top desk 55

Antony Todd 35

anxiety xiv, 6, 32, 115

apothecary chest 98, 99

appraiser 45

AptDeco 14, 15, 80, 82

architectural style 21, 23

arousal 48

art 15, 37

asymmetry 67, 137

Athena Calderone 35

attention deficit hyperactivity disorder (ADHD) 9

Attention restoration theory 48

auctioneer 14, 46, 78, 105

auditioning rugs online 133

autism spectrum disorder (ASD) 9

autonomy 5

B

backsplash 93

Bailey turned legs 42

Bandura, A. 5

barrel back armchair 82

baseboard heating 139

bay windows 103

Beatles 102

bedding 112

Beethoven, Ludwig van, Sonata No. 14, in C Sharp Minor, Op. 27, No. 2, Moonlight 90

belly basket 157

Benessent Design xiv, xv, 37

Benjamin Moore 23
    Advanced Interior Paint 154
    At Sea 51
    Aura Bath & Spa 118
    Bath Salts 118
    Blossom Tint 24, 25
    First Snowfall 66
    French Beret 24, 25
    Indi Go-Go 154
    Pink Essence 126
    Silver Mist 65
    Simply White 25
    website 15, 21, 24, 94, 95
    Wispy Green 97

Biffi Transport LLC 81

birds 33, 48

black and white geometric tiles 97

blackout curtains 112

Blenko Glass Company 155

blood-brain barrier 115

blossoming dogwood 149

blue light 113

body of the house 22, 23, 24, 25

boucle 131

boundaries 6

boxwood plants 22

boxwood topiary 137

brain health xv, 112, 113

brass towel bar 155

breakfast nook 103

brick wall 23

broaden the color palette 94

Bunny Mellon 35

C

cacophony 133

candelabra 67

canopy beds xiv

carbon monoxide 39

care facilities 32

caregiver 7

Carolina Leg Company 42

carved dragon lion armchair 87

center island 92

cerebral reserve 11

chandeliers 76, 77

checkered cutting board 155

China 55, 87

Chinese Carved Dragon Chair 87

Chopin, Etude No. 12 in C Minor, op. 25, Ocean 90

Claire Tabouret 36

Clare Paint
    Flatiron 73
    Frozen 145
    Goodnight Moon 97
    On Point 41, 73, 139
    Whipped 46, 118, 139, 147
    Windy City 46

classical architecture 24

Cleopatra (1963) 117

clothing and household items 14

clutter 9, 13, 37, 45, 58, 98, 113

coffee table 49, 50, 69, 76, 80

cognitive decline 10, 114

cognitive strength 115

color-field painting 37, 49

Colors2U.net 152

columns 21, 23, 25, 103

combustible gas vapors 38

comfort 15

comfort and safety xv

common humanity 37

communicate 6

concrete artichokes 28

confidence 6, 35, 36

connections 34

contractor-grade mirror 73

contrast 23

control 7, 32

convergent thinking 17

cool colors 15, 145

Corian® countertops 93

Corian® Solid Surface 151, 152

Corinthian columns 40

cotton sateen tablecloth 44

Covid-19 pandemic 10, 32

Crate & Barrel 64

creative challenge 16

creative process 37

creative struggles 37

creativity 5, 7, 17, 37

creativity and intellectual activity 47

critical thinking 5

crown molding 76, 105

cultured marble 116

cupboard and drawer knobs 95

cupboards 154

curtains 78, 155

curved lines 26

D

daily workouts 113

dampen noise 112

dance 37

Danish xv

DAP FastN Final Lightweight Spackling 118

David J. Linden Ph.D. 113

Deborah Finco Art 60

decision-making 13, 16

decluttering 14, 101

default mode network 16

delays and frustrations 17

dementia 10

depression xiv, 32, 115

depth 67

design 37

Dialectical Behavior Therapy (DBT) 137

dimmer switch 9, 101

disengaged 8

distracted 13

divergent thinking 16

dogs 139

Double Coverage Seaglass by Carole Fabric 88

Dragon Chair 87

Dragon Lion Armchair 87

drama 40, 67, 97, 152, 154, 157

driveway roundabout 23, 28

dumpster 14

dusting 58

E

eBay 14, 15, 44, 99, 114, 132, 153, 155

electricity 38

Élisabeth Louise Vigée Le Brun 107

emotional regulation 5

emotions 115

Empire shape 109

encouragement 6

endocannabinoids 115

endorphins 115

energy 13, 36, 78, 84

enmeshed 6

enriched environment xiv, xv, 10

Erin Ashley 107

essential developmental tasks 5

Etsy 15, 57, 83, 95, 105

evolve 40

executive control network 16

executive functioning xiv, xv, 8, 9, 13

exercise equipment 113

exposure to nature 48

exterior brick wall 28

eye 15, 17, 23, 24, 30, 35, 36, 37, 49, 82, 83, 97, 133, 135, 137, 145, 154

Ezequiel Farca 35

F

fabric backdrop 42, 44
façade 20
Facebook 14, 59, 78, 101, 152
face-to-face contact 10
family caregivers 2, 160
family photos 58
Farrow & Ball 23
fascia 25
faux pleats 134
faux water lily 155
fireplace 67
flames 39
fleece blanket 50
Florian Marquardt 36
focal point 49, 67, 97, 154, 157
focus xiv, 5, 13, 37, 47, 101
foyer 40
fractals 48, 139
freedom 7, 36
free technology 15
fun 17, 22, 40, 69, 113
furnaces 38

G

galley kitchen 150, 154, 155, 157, 160
gas leak 38
gas leak and carbon monoxide detector 38
geometric-patterned rug 49
Georgian architecture 24
Giovanni Fattori 76, 148
glass 15, 49, 80, 155

gold-veined black marble 72
good nutrition xiv, xv
Google Docs 160
grandfather clock 105
Greek Ionic columns 76
Greek Revival 23, 24
grow 30, 37

H

Half Price Drapes 110
healthy meals 12
healthy mental functioning 4, 12
healthy personality 5
healthy relationships 5
heat gun 117
high-humidity environments 118
HI-MACSÆ Solid Surface 152
hippocampus 115
Hollywood Blvd 108
Home Armor Mildew Stain Remover 118
Home Depot 152
hospice care 3
Hugues Magen 35
human brain 10, 24
hygge xv

I

ikat 49, 69, 110
illness 6
imagination 15, 16
imperfections xv, 17, 141
impermanence xv
impulses 9
inflammation 12

insomnia 2

intellectual and creative stimulation xv

intellectual and emotional needs xv

interior design xiv, 4, 7, 10, 13, 16

Into the Deep Blue 59, 60

invisible threats 38

Ionic columns 77

ionization 39

isolation 32, 34

J

James + James Furniture 42

Japanese xv

Johns Hopkins University 113

jute rug 68, 105, 133, 155

K

Kate Spade tote 123

Keurig coffee maker 159

kitchen 12, 92, 103

kitchen island 97

kitchen trash bin 157

knickknacks 45

Korea 106

L

laminate countertops 150

language 33, 37

La Rotonda di Palmieri 76

layering 67

Leadcheck Disposable Non-Staining Lead Detection Swabs 105

Leanne Ford 35

learning 6, 115

Led Zeppelin 90

Leesa Sapira mattress 112, 140, 147

literature 33

lithium battery 38, 39

Little Shop of Horrors (1960) 156

local library 14

lockdown 10

locus of control 7

loneliness 10

LRV (Light Reflectance Value) 24

M

machine washable rug 121

mahogany ètagére 75, 76

mantle 59, 60, 63, 66, 67, 105, 133, 135, 136, 137

marble floor 40

Marie Antoinette 107

Mark Rothko iv, 37, 49, 66

mastery 35

Matthew Harris 35

medical equipment 14

medical supplies 14

mementos 36, 63

memories 36

memory 11, 115

memory loss 10

mental deterioration 10

mental equilibrium 10

mental exercise 17

mental fatigue 48

mental health v, 7, 10, 13

mental health goals xv

mental health therapist 4

meta 37
mid-century modern 68, 84, 86, 103, 131, 132, 139, 147
mildew 118
minimalism 50, 67
mirror 67, 78
missions abroad 14
modern furniture 15
Modern Greek Revival 23
mold 118
molding 46, 47, 124
Monica Calderon 35
movement 84
moviemaking 37
mudcloth 128
Murano 155
Murder at The Naughty Cabbage, L.M. Snowe 160
music 37, 91, 101

N

natural gas 39
natural light 46, 47, 78
nature 24, 147
nerve cell connections 115
nerve cell growth 115
neurogenesis 113
neuroplasticity 10
new beginning 37
nonlinear approach 16
normal aging 114

O

older appliances 38
online activities 9

organizing 16
overeating 13
overstimulation 9
oxidative stress 12
oxytocin 50

P

padded headboard 140, 141
Page, J., Plant, R., Bonham, J. Kashmir 90
paint 16, 17
painting 37, 141
paint remover 29
Parkinsons disease 2, 3
patio 78
pedestals 28
pendant lamps 154
pendant light fixtures 101
Performance count aka rub count 89
personal space 6, 35
pet resort 139
photoelectric sensors 39
photography 37
photos 33, 36, 63
physical decline 10
physical illness 32
piano 76, 89, 91
pillars 23, 26
Pinterest 15, 16, 35, 94, 150, 154
plan and organize xiv
planning 16
plant 155
planter boxes 22, 26
playful 17, 40
pleated lamp shade 109

portico 21, 23, 25, 103

Portrait of Countess Nathalie Golovine 108

Poshmark 132, 135, 144

poshmark.com 14, 15

post-exercise high 115

Pottery Barn 132, 144

power in odd numbers 67

power sander 29, 118

PPG Paints 23

prefrontal cortex 9

primary caregiver 5

privacy screen 4

probate 3

problem-solving 5, 16

prodigy 89

professional counseling v

professional designers 35

psychology 137

Pythagoras 117

Q

quality of life 13

R

Rachmaninoff, Piano Concerto No. 2, op. 21 90

radical acceptance 137

radon 39

reflect light 78

regulate our emotions xiv

resilience 5

resilience capacity 11

RH (RH, formerly Restoration Hardware) 82

risks 6

Robert Louis Stevenson vi

Rodgers, Richard, and Oscar Hammerstein. Youll Never Walk Alone 90

roll top desk 103

Romabio Classico Limewash 28

Roman window shades 139, 147

room darkening shades 112

round breakfast table 103

round mirror 148

round throw pillow 83, 144

rowing machine 113

rub count 89

rug 15

rugs-direct.com 134

Russian nesting dolls 48

S

Safavieh 78

safe space 6

safety 38

safety poles 23

salience network 16

Samplize 23

scale 69, 76, 103

sculpture 15, 37, 44

sectional sofa 47, 50, 55

self-discipline 5

self-efficacy 5

self-esteem 13

senior living facilities 10

sense of mastery 5

sensory processing disorder 9

sentimental 24

sharp angles 22

Sherwin Williams 23

Shibori 43, 44

shower head 149

shutters 22, 23, 24, 25

sidelights 23

simplicity xv

single pinch pleat 78

sleep xiv, xv, 9, 11, 91, 112

sleep 142

smartphone 38

Smart Strip Advanced Paint Remover by Dumond 29

smoke detectors 39

smoldering materials 39

social connection 11, 32

social distancing 33

social isolation 10

social media 35

social needs 32

social stimulation 10

social support xiv, 6, 10, 32

solid surface countertop 152

solitude 33

Sondheim, Stephen. Send in the Clowns 90

soothing textures 15

Spoonflower 43, 44, 106, 111

Spotify 90, 113

square embellished grommet curtains 147

squirrels 48

steamer 117

stimulation 6, 15

straight lines 22, 26

stress 9, 11, 13, 16, 17, 101

stress response 32

successful aging 112

sunken bathtub 117

sunlight 147

Sylvia Wyler (boathousepottery.com) 69

symmetry 23, 24

T

tambour 103

tambour-look pedestal table 103

Target 76, 104

tassels 78

TCP 118

texture 50

theater 37

therapeutic 101

Thigh Master 113, 114

thrift stores 15

throw pillow 15, 49, 57, 83

Thuma bed 140, 141, 147

toile 130, 131, 133, 136, 137

tole chandelier 105

topiary 67, 69

transom 20, 23

trauma 6

trees 48

trim 23

turned sofa legs 86

U

uncluttered environment 101

United States Naval Academy 89

upholstered bench with two drawers 147

upholstered furniture 14, 78, 112

urns 23, 26, 27

used mattresses 139
US Navy 87

V

velvet 50
Vietnam Veterans of America (VVA) 14, 46
vintage-looking clockface 97
vinyl adhesive tiles 154
vinyl tile stickers 95
vinyl wallpaper 116, 117
vision 35, 94
voice 7, 30, 35, 36, 37
Volatile organic compounds (VOCs) 41

W

wabi-sabi xv, 141
waffle weave duvet cover 139, 147
Wagner Spraytech Wallpaper Steamer 40
wallpaper adhesive 116, 117
wall sconce 118, 146
warm colors 15, 145
water heaters 38
Waverly Savoy 149
weighted blankets 9, 112
well-being xiv, 7, 34
wicker chair 50
wicker shade 155
wicker storage baskets with lids 99
Wi-Fi 55, 56, 159
Williams, Pharrell. Happy 90
window 147, 154
wingback chairs xiv
work from home 7
writing 37

Wyzenbeek Method 89

Z

Zinsser Mold Killing Primer 118
Zoom calls 33

www.ingramcontent.com/pod-product-compliance
Lightning Source LLC
Chambersburg PA
CBHW051514110526
44582CB00008B/158